Out of India

TIM PIGOTT-SMITH

Out of India

Duckworth

First published in 1986 by
Constable & Company Ltd
Second edition 1997 by
Gerald Duckworth & Co. Ltd.
The Old Piano Factory
48 Hoxton Square, London N1 6PB
Tel: 0171 729 5986
Fax: 0171 729 0015

© 1986 by Tim Pigott-Smith

A catalogue record for this book is available
from the British Library

ISBN 0 7156 2790 2

Typeset by Rowland Typsetting Ltd
Bury St Edmunds, Suffolk
Printed in Great Britain by
Page Bros (Norwich) Ltd, Norwich

Contents

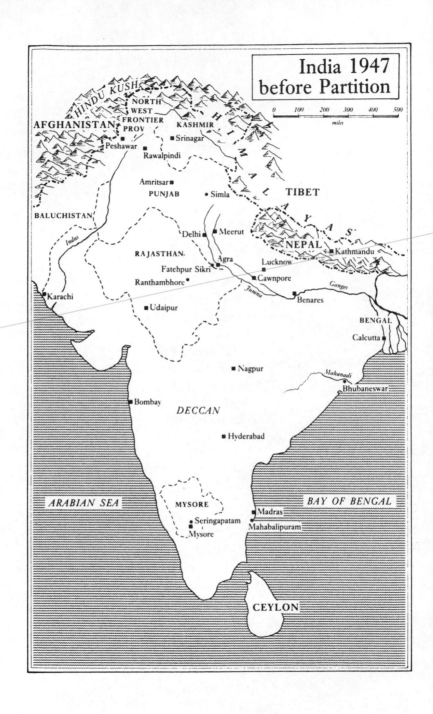

India 1947 before Partition

Foreword

In January 1982, I flew to India to begin filming my contribution to *The Jewel in the Crown*. It was my first trip to India, a very privileged, carefully scheduled trip, which took me to Delhi, Udaipur, Bombay, Bangalore, Mysore, Simla and Kashmir. It provided our camera with very diverse backgrounds: from the crowded street life of a Rajasthani village and the desert stretches beyond its crumbling city walls, to the fabulous snowy Himalayan backdrop that encircles Simla: from the burnt southern landscapes of Mysore to the mountain-ringed, willow-fringed lakes of Kashmir. Independently I visited Agra, Kathmandu, and the jungle of Ranthambore.

During my stay I kept a diary – memories of the filming, the locations, the crew, the production-team; in a word, the job. But in addition, I found myself using the extra time at my disposal to record some fairly detailed stories, bits of history, passages of description, of sensation and impression. I realised that in the then distant wintry days to come in Manchester, where we had a further year's shooting in which to complete the series, I might well have need of 'reminders' of the heat, the smells, the warm wind, the woodsmoke, the cow-dung fires, the fun and the frustration, the pleasures and difficulties.

It is to this twelve month period during which I wrote up my diary, and read anything I came across about India, that I owe both a play, based on Francis Yeats-Brown's extraordinary book *Bengal Lancer*, and an anthology, which I gradually put together with my wife Pamela Miles, and our dear friend Roger Pringle, an anthologist of great experience. It is the diary and the anthology which form the basis of this book.

The anthology is the basis of a programme which Pam and I

used to perform with Zia Mohyeddin; we were aided by the invaluable accompaniment of Viram Jasani's sitar. Audiences seem genuinely to be transported to India by our efforts, and I am delighted that my own fascination has been successfully transformed into something capable of capturing an audience's imagination; if it were also to encourage any understanding of India herself, and, more importantly, of those Indians who live amongst us, I should be doubly gratified, but first and foremost this collection is an entertainment.

The anthology is put together in such a way as to lead you through a series of impressions and feelings in the style of a collage. The juxtaposition and the accumulative effect of the pieces is what I hope will help you to discover and ultimately 'sense' something of India.

I am no writer: that is why I have selected other people's words. Nor can I claim any originality of insight. What binds the material together is my own sense of intrigue, for I am under the spell of India, and long to discover more of our countries' inexplicably, inextricably interwoven lives. I hope that through this book my pleasures and interests reach you, my enthusiasms infect you, and India touches you.

Dedication

In expanding and enlarging the anthology for the page, I have allowed my relationships and personal interests to emerge more than would be proper in a shared performance, and in keeping with that personal note, I wish to dedicate this book to three Indians whom I met during the filming. I am still in touch with one of them – Narendra Singh. He is the brother of the Maharana of Udaipur, and owns a hotel outside the town where he stables the horses which we used in our filming. He had a kindness and grace, an acceptance and generosity which charmed me into India, and our rides through the hills to his lotus-lake, as he taught me how to control the fiery horse I had to ride, and talked of the India of his childhood, are quite unforgettable.

One of his hotel staff was a boy called Kooba, to whom I gave a small amount of money. He was one of thirteen that his family was unable to support. He was then eleven years old, the size of an English seven year old, and he worshipped Narendra, returning his master's generosity in taking him on, with an affecting keenness.

At our hotel in Udaipur, there was a waiter – B. J. Bannerjee – of whom we were all very fond. Sadly I have lost touch with him; I suspect he has moved to another hotel, and that he no longer receives my increasingly irregular letters. His letters, addressed to 'Dear Brother Tim Pigott-Smith', for he was a Christian, no longer arrive upon my door-mat. But I wish they would, for I miss them sorely.

You will meet these people, dotted among the coming pages. But there is only one way, and one place to start, and that is . . . in the beginning.

Birth

Creation Hymn from *The Rig Veda* (*c.* 600 BC)

There was neither non-existence nor existence then; there was neither the realm of space nor the sky which is beyond. What stirred? Where? In whose protection? Was there water, bottomlessly deep?

There was neither death nor immortality then. There was no distinguishing sign of night nor of day. That one breathed, windless, by its own impulse. Other than that there was nothing beyond.

Darkness was hidden by darkness in the beginning; with no distinguishing sign, all this was water. The life force that was covered with emptiness, that one arose through the power of heat.

Desire came upon that one in the beginning; that was the first seed of mind. Poets seeking in their heart with wisdom found the bond of existence in non-existence.

Their cord was extended across. Was there below? Was there above? There were seed-placers; there were powers. There was impulse beneath; there was giving-forth above.

Who really knows? Who will here proclaim it? Whence was it produced? Whence is this creation? The gods came afterwards, with the creation of this universe. Who then knows whence it has arisen?

Whence this creation has arisen – perhaps it formed itself, or perhaps it did not – the one who looks down on it, in the highest heaven, only he knows – or perhaps he does not know.

from *Passage to India* by E. M. Forster (1924)

The Ganges, though flowing from the foot of Vishnu and through Siva's hair, is not an ancient stream. Geology, looking further than religion, knows of a time when neither the river nor the

Himalayas that nourished it existed, and an ocean flowed over the holy places of Hindustan. The mountains arose, their debris silted up the ocean, the gods took their seats on them and contrived the river, and the India we call immemorial came into being. But India is really far older. In the days of the prehistoric ocean the southern part of the peninsula already existed, and the high places of Dravidia have been land since land began, and have seen on the one side the sinking of a continent that joined them to Africa, and on the other the upheaval of the Himalayas from a sea. They are older than anything in the world. No water has ever covered them, and the sun who has watched them for countless aeons may still discern in their outlines forms that were his before our globe was torn from his bosom. If flesh of the sun's flesh is to be touched anywhere, it is here, among the incredible antiquity of these hills.

The Gateway of India by Alan Ross (1973)

The first addictive smell
And that curiously sated light
In which dhows and islands float
Lining the air with spices.

The beginning and end
of India, birth and death,
The bay curved as a kukri
And on Malabar Hill the vultures,
Like seedy waiters, scooping the crumbs
Off corpses.

[14]

'The beginning and end
of India, Birth and Death',

That line echoes through my mind.

From my diary . . .

Since before a time that I can imagine from my western
viewpoint, entire civilisations have come and gone in India. The
country has been a receptacle into which kings and rulers,
religions and philosophers, whole empires, long before the
British, have thrown their influence as into a huge melting-pot.
And India seems to have accepted a bit of all of them.
Acceptance appears to be the best and worst part of its national
character.

Think of Tamburlaine – Marlowe's Scythian Shepherd.

What, think'st thou Tamburlaine esteems thy gold?
I'll make the kings of India, ere I die,
Offer their mines, to sue for peace to me,
And dig for treasure to appease my wrath.

And he did, too, for Tamburlaine the Great overthrew Delhi in
1398, and established the Moghul Empire. They ruled in Delhi
until Akbar the Great transferred his court to the newly-built
city of Fatehpur Sikri, close to Agra in the 1570's.

At about this time, of course, English colonial expansion was
also looking east, and not long after King James I sent the
ambassador Sir Thomas Roe to negotiate with the then emperor
Jehangir. While he was there Roe met an extraordinary
Englishman who was buccaneering his way around India –
Thomas Coryat. . .

from *The Lord of the Dance*,
being the adventures of Thomas Coryat, an English surgeon.
by Robin Lloyd-Jones (1983)

In the current of humanity that flowed by, there now appeared the floating wreckage, beggars by the thousand. They shuffled, hopped, crawled or dragged themselves along, displaying their withered limbs, their amputations and deformities. In all, I would estimate that this rabble, which stretched to the horizon, outnumbered the soldiers who had gone before by ten to one. They had been filling the highway for nearly three hours when an ox cart approached the temple.

Inside the covered cart a woman was screaming. Although we doctors are expected to leave matters of childbirth to the women-folk, there is no mistaking the sound of a woman in labour. Beside the cart, a man ran in circles, beating frantically on a drum as if to drown the noise. A small, fat figure, whom I took to be a child, seized the rope that ran through the nose-ring of the two oxen and began to lead them off the road. A gaunt, hollow-chested man, driving the cart, cursed him and lashed at him with a whip, but the small figure hung on, and the cart jolted to a halt beside the temple.

It has always seemed to me ironical that the greatest danger most of us ever face in this world is the moment of our entry into it. Certainly it is not a matter that should be left to the care of old crones whose ways are steeped in superstition, magic and other erroneous suppositions.

More screams emanated from the cart. The men fidgeted and avoided each other's eye. Between fits of coughing, the driver hurled abuse into the cart. 'Hurry up, you stupid girl! Can't you be quicker about it? Already we're being left behind!'

I stood up. 'Is anyone with the woman?' They ignored me. 'I am a physician,' I announced.

The news was received with indifference. The driver, a man older than the others, eyed me coldly.

[16]

'These things are best left to the gods and the stars. She will be all right. Only last week she consulted an astrologer who foretold a healthy boy. And it was only this morning she made *puja* to the goddess Parvati . . . So, you see, there is nothing to be done . . .' He broke into a fit of coughing, before adding: 'Except, of course, that the army marches into the distance and we shall be left at the roadside here without the safety of numbers to protect us, or an audience to pay for our performance . . . Hurry up, girl!'

A cry of pain answered him.

'I think I had better take a look at her,' I said, edging towards the cart.

He flicked his whip in front of my face. 'We have no money to waste on doctors and their useless nostrums.'

'I make no charge!' I retorted sharply.

He gave me a hard, suspicious stare, then lowered his whip.

The girl lay on a pile of old rags. I guessed that she was no more than fourteen or fifteen. She had a thin face with large, expressive eyes. Her left nostril held a jewelled nose-ring. Rivers of sweat had caused the red *talik* mark on her brow to smear and run. The atmosphere was oppressive. Incense smouldered in a dish. A lamp with three wicks smoked near the curtain, which I had pulled aside on entering. One of the wicks blew out. She whined in a shrill, frightened voice: 'Quick! Light it again. Don't you know anything? An even number brings bad luck!'

I crouched beside her. She would not let me touch her. She screamed at me to go away. But, when the pain started again, she clutched my hand and made no objection when I wiped her brow.

I talked to the girl, Mohini, trying to gain her confidence, trying to keep her thoughts from her pain and fear. I told her my name and a little about myself.

'How many wives do you have?' she asked.

'None.' Perhaps it was true in the eyes of the Church, but it felt like a lie.

'Are there no women with you?' There was anxiety in her voice. I shook my head, and she started a nervous monologue. Which

[17]

sari should she put on when it was over? Should it be the blue one with the silver border, or the green and yellow one? Yes, the blue one, she thought. Did I like her bracelets? They had been given to her by an admirer when they had danced at Jaipur. No, perhaps the green and yellow one would be better. She gabbled faster and faster.

'Is this your first baby?' I interrupted.

She nodded. 'I shall call him Prajapathi,' she said. 'For it was by the god Prajapathi that he was conceived.'

She related how the troupe – they were itinerant dancers – had encamped near the cave temple of Revari. In the darkness of the inmost cave, beside the altar, an echoing voice had spoken to her saying that, because of her devotion, he, Prajapathi, would assume the mortal form of a Brahmin priest and lie with her. She, naturally, had consented to this most holy act. Somewhere in the course of this pathetically naïve tale, I discovered that the troupe was from Rajasthan and that the ill-tempered driver, who kept shouting through the cart's bamboo screens, was Gampopa, their *nayaka* or dancing-master, the leader of the troupe.

Mohini's hand tightened on mine. Her back was arched, her knees drawn up. A gush of greenish fluid soaked the rags beneath her. Many a midwife have I questioned concerning all that happens behind the closed doors. Occasionally, when things have gone badly wrong, I have been summoned to fumble under the sheets and drag forth a dead infant, or to ease the last hours of an exhausted and dying mother. But here, in the stuffy, dirty little cart, I, a doctor of some experience, was about to be initiated into the mysteries of the human female giving birth to her young. Mohini gave a sharp cry. I cursed myself for a pompous ass. Here was no specimen to be studied unfeelingly, but a girl fighting her loneliness and fear and smiling bravely at me.

'Khorat,' she said, attempting my name, 'when the time comes, be sure to note the exact position of the sun in the sky. Upon this depends the accuracy of his horoscope.'

I gave her a sip of water. It must have been close on midday, judging by the heat inside the cart. I became aware of the silence on the highway. Gampopa was coughing again ... Mohini lay back, listening, a pleased smile on her face. Suddenly she sat up.

'They didn't draw a circle round the cart!'

I stared at her.

'A circle!' she shouted. 'To avert the evil eye!' She fell back with a groan. 'I wish there was another woman here.'

'Surely there's more than one female in a dancing troupe.'

'The others were in the front cart. They won't have stopped. If we don't dance, we don't eat – that's a saying of ours.'

Her face screwed up in pain. 'A circle!' she panted.

I stuck my head outside and suggested that somebody might draw a circle in the dust.

'We men cannot go near the cart without defiling ourselves,' said Gampopa, who had dismounted and was standing apart with the others. 'And think of the expense!' he exclaimed. 'Think what it would cost in offerings at the temple to atone for such uncleanness.'

The intervals between Mohini's pains were becoming shorter, I observed. It was important that my patient be in a calm state of mind. I climbed out of the cart and scratched a circle on the ground round the vehicle. Frog watched this performance with glee, making some foolish pretence that I subscribed to such superstitious nonsense.

Mohini began to hum in a nervous high-pitched way. It was a popular song of love which we had heard up and down the highway for the last month or more. Her song suddenly lurched into a long, agonized note.

'It's coming!' she gasped. She was breathing hard, in great sobbing gulps.

I pulled her sari up to her waist. Perhaps I was aware of her slender legs, the smoothness of her thighs, but only fleetingly, before the marvel of new life emerging absorbed me totally. Beyond the orifice of her organ of generation, an oval shape was visible. She rested, panting, soaked in sweat, clinging hard to my hand, still jerkily humming shreds of her ridiculous song. The blood-smeared oval shape moved forward, parting the lips of the vulva, stretching them till surely they must split. At first I was not sure what I was seeing. Then I realised it was the top of the baby's head. It slipped back and the lips closed again.

'I'm tired, Khorat! I'm so tired!'

'Not long now.'

It was coming again. This time the whole head appeared, face downwards. The baby let out an indignant yell.

'Well, Mohini, he's going to have a lot to say for himself! He's only just got his head out and he's telling us what he thinks of the world!'

There was a pause. I could hear the oxen snuffing and stamping. With a miraculous spiral movement, the shoulders emerged. I was shouting with excitement:

'Come on! Come on!'

Ignorant, superstitious, courageous, wonderful Mohini gathered her strength and pushed, gave a loud cry and was delivered of a child.

I held up the baby by the heels. An ugly little creature, covered in blood and white grease, for all the world like a freshly skinned rabbit.

'How is my son? Tell me how he is, Khoratji!'

'Yes, you have a son, Mohini; a beautiful boy.'

I tied off the umbilical cord with thread from my bag and severed mother from child. I cleaned the baby as best I could with a rag and tepid water, wondering at the strength of the grip on my finger. He mewed like a kitten.

'Prajapathi!' Mohini called softly. 'Prajapathi,' she murmured, holding out her hands. As she took the infant into her arms, her face softened. Fresh tears ran down her wet cheeks. Did ever pain and joy so sweetly mingle?

Tenderly she anointed her son's head with clarified butter and smeared his little body with castor oil and saffron powder. To

me, the young Prajapathi looked in a worse mess than before
I had cleaned him, but Mohini was happy and began to sing
again.

Outside, in the blinding glare, I handed a bloodstained bundle
to Gampopa.

'This needs to be buried deep, where the jackals cannot devour
it.'

'Oh, so it died then. Just as well. Dancers are better without
these encumbrances.'

'No, Gampopa, the baby Prajapathi lives. This is the . . .' – I
didn't know the word for afterbirth – '. . . just the rags she lay on,
Gampopa. But Mohini says it would be an evil omen were the wild
animals to dig them up.'

To My Daughter Rookzain by Keki Daruwalla (1982)

> Three years and then again
> the uterus flowered.
>
> Lights reeled for her
> and then blacked off
> as they drew you
> from the weedbed of the womb.
>
> Then you cried:
> a lung of light
> in a dark room
> and she came back.
>
> Two vaccine-marks
> sprout bulbous on your arm
> which lies over my shoulder
> halfway across my back,

and as you turn warmer
and heavier in my arms
I know that sleep has caught up with you.

Supple-boned fledgeling
you are all gristle, soft-chalk bone
and spiny shadow,
your looks quick with startled birds.

Snug in a forest of syllables
without which the winds prowl
without which the winds howl
   but cannot enter.

May you live for ever
   in the house of words.

But if you falter, blind with rain
don't panic, you'll find an arm
brown as bark
and when you reach for the bark
may you find the flowers thereon.

While wandering you may hitchhike
through the strangest lands
but when you rest
have known things around you.

Look fresh, like a rain-washed leaf
with a spray of light on it
and may your breath be spiked
as now, with the tang
of mint and clove and cinnamon.

from *The Jewel in the Crown* by Paul Scott (1966)

The death of Daphne Manners and the birth of Parvati

from a letter of her aunt, Lady Ethel Manners, written from her houseboat in Kashmir, 1943.

She died of peritonitis. For a couple of days afterwards I wouldn't even look at the child. I'd seen it cut out. Krishnamurti let me watch. I was dressed up like a nurse in theatre in a white gown, with a mask over my mouth and nostrils. I needed to see this side of life. I'd never have forgiven myself for being too faint-hearted to watch. When it began I thought I'd never stand it. It seemed obscene, like opening a can – which isn't obscene but is when the can is a human abdomen. But then when the can was open and I saw what they were lifting out I felt I was being born again myself. It was a miracle and it made you realise that no miracle is beautiful because it exists on a plane of experience where words like beauty have no meaning whatsoever.

It also meant absolutely nothing to me that the curious knotted little bundle of flesh that was lifted out of Daphne – (perhaps prised is a better word because with their long rubber gloves on they seemed to have to search for and encourage it to emerge) – was obviously *not* the same colour as its mother. The difference in colour was subtle, so subtle that were it not for one particular recollection I'd now be persuaded that the fact that the difference between them meant nothing was due to my failing to notice one at the time. But I did notice it. The particular recollection I have is of thinking, Yes – I see – the father *was* dark-skinned. But at the time this caused no emotional response. I noted it and then forgot it. I only remembered it when Daphne was dead and they tried to show me the child to take my mind off things. But that wasn't the reason I rejected it. I rejected it because in the state of mind I was in I blamed it for killing Daphne.

If anything its Indian-ness was what first made me feel pity for it and start thinking of it as 'she'.

Thus Daphne dies, but into the world comes Parvati, a tragic blend of England and India.

From my diary . . .

On June 7th 1631, Mumtaz Mahal died in childbirth. She was having her fourteenth child by Shah Jehan (son of Jehangir) who, out of his pain and loss, built the Taj Mahal in her memory. One of Shah Jehan's surviving children has a less well-known, but touching epitaph, which she composed by herself

> Let nothing but
> Green conceal me.
> Grass is the best covering
> for the poor,
> the humble, the transitory
> Jehanara
> daughter of the Emperor
> Shah Jehan.

The story of Jehanara brings us to the concluding passage of this opening section. It concerns a birth of a rather different kind.

from *Bengal Lancer* by Francis Yeats-Brown (1930)

The story begins by Jehanara's maid upsetting an oil lamp in the palace of Shah Jehan. Jehanara tried to save her, and in doing so she scorched herself about the face and hands. Shah Jehan was in a fever of anxiety about his daughter: the aesthete as well as the parent in him demanded that the best physician in his Empire must attend its loveliest princess.

Thus it happened that Gabriel Broughton, the surgeon of the English factory at Surat, arrived at Agra. Although hampered by the etiquette of *purdah* (he was only allowed to feel his patient's pulse from behind a curtain) he not only cured Jehanara but saved her beauty flawless. As reward, he would take nothing for himself, but asked that a charter should be given to the East India Company to trade in Bengal.

These are the threads of *karma* that go to the making of ant-heaps and Empires: a clumsy slave-girl, a kind princess, and an altruistic doctor who asked for the charter on which the British built Calcutta.

Into Jehanara's history is woven by the twists and quirks of fate, our own Imperial destinies. But for her, British India would have had a different birth.

Childhood

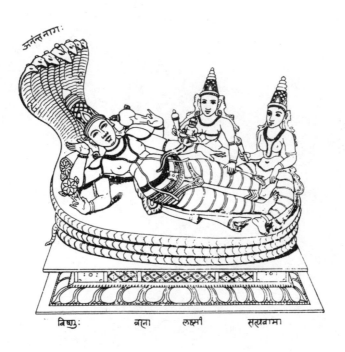

अनंतनागः

विष्णुः   बाना   लक्ष्मी   सत्यभामा

From my diary . . .

On one of my early bicycle rides through the seething narrow
streets of the village of Udaipur, I was adopted by a diminutive,
nippy, excitable young imp of a lad full of life and fun. He
offered to tend my bicycle whilst I was buying something inside
a shop. His name was Dinesh. Thereafter I could not get rid of
him, but he turned out to be so companionable a child, that in
the end I didn't want to. More importantly he had enough
English for us to communicate. He rode alongside me, through
the bazaar, telling me which shops were good, which bad, and as
I was looking for gifts he took me to the grandly-named
Jagdeesh Emporium, partly for my sake, but partly also, to cheer
up his friends – the three boys who owned the shop, whose
mother had just died.
    'You filming star. Yes. I know. You come. This make them
very happy.'
    It was a very good shop. I thought I paid fair prices for some
antique miniature bronzes, and the boys did seem happier
when I left, although I hadn't spent a great deal of money.
Consequently I felt that Dinesh – unlike many of the other lads
who tried to take me over – was *bona fide*, special. When we
parted I offered him a couple of rupees, which he refused with
horror. 'You my friend!', he said.
    I asked if he had a job. (Perhaps he was much older than he
looked; it was very easy to be misled by their size and childish
charm.) He shook his head. 'Too young', he said, 'I go school'.
Indeed, he did have schoolbooks under his arm.
    I said that he would make me happy if he took the small
amount offered, but he was adamant. He also hinted that he had
many irons in the fire, and really did not need the money. It is
more than likely that the shop boys would give him commission
for taking me to their shop, but nevertheless, this refusal of
money was most unusual.
    Whenever I biked into town on one of my many trips – to find

[29]

a silversmith who could engrave, to find a picture-framer, to buy flowers or scent – I would think to myself, 'I wish old Dinesh was here', and there he would be. It never failed. He was a magic boy, an enthusiast. Life seemed lighter when he was with you. The other lads were envious and bitched him.

'Him bad boy, sahib. You come. Me and my friend. Show you better places. Him. Bad'. But I had no need of anyone other than Dinesh and he never once took money from me.

'You like school?' I asked him one day.

'OK Sahib, OK. One day' he confided 'I show you my special school'.

As one of my strangest memories of India – to be found later in the book – concerns Dinesh, please, remember him.

Dinesh's frantic urban existence is very different from the timeless peace and rural calm described here by Hermann Hesse . . .

from *Siddhartha* by Hermann Hesse (1970)

In the shade of the house, in the sunshine on the river bank by the boats, in the shade of the sallow wood and the fig tree, Siddhartha, the handsome Brahmin's son grew up with his friend Govinda.

The sun browned his slender shoulders on the river bank, while bathing at the holy ablutions, at the holy sacrifices. Shadows passed across his eyes in the mango grove, while his mother sang, during his father's teaching, when with the learned men.

There was happiness in his father's heart because of his son who was intelligent and thirsty for knowledge; he saw him growing up to be a great learned man, a priest, a prince among Brahmins.

There was pride in his mother's breast when she saw him

walking, sitting down, rising; Siddhartha – strong, handsome, supple-limbed, greeting her with complete grace.

Love stirred in the hearts of the young Brahmin's daughters when Siddhartha walked through the streets of the town, with his lofty brow, his king-like eyes and his slim figure.

Govinda, his friend, the Brahmin's son, loved him more than anybody else. He loved Siddhartha's eyes and clear voice. He loved the way he walked, his complete grace of movement; he loved everything that Siddhartha did and said, and above all he loved his intellect, his fine ardent thoughts, his strong will, his high vocation.

That was how everybody loved Siddhartha. He delighted them and made them happy.

There is a famous Hindi book containing many, many stories written down in about 200 BC, but probably dating from much earlier as they all derived from the oral tradition. A wise old Brahmin collected these delightful tales together and the young Siddhartha may have heard them either recounted by a travelling storyteller in the shade of a tree by the river, or possibly read to him from the book; fables such as this one . . .

The Brahmin's Dream adapted by Lee Wyndham

There once lived a Brahmin whose name was Savarakipana, which means 'born to be poor', and this he was. One day, as he was begging for his daily food, a kind man gave him a bag of barley meal. When the Brahmin had used a portion of this for his supper, he found that there was enough left over for the next day, and perhaps the next. To keep it safe he put the barley meal into a clay pot and hung the pot from a nail on the wall above his bed.

While he prepared for sleep he could not keep from looking at the pot of meal since it was most unusual for him to have any food left over. The thought was so exciting that he began to daydream.

'If there were famine in this country,' he said to himself, 'I could easily get one hundred rupees for this pot of barley meal. With this money I could buy a couple of goats, male and female. Every six months my goats would bear some kids. In a few years I would have a whole flock of goats.

'By selling the kids I would get enough money to buy a bull and a cow. With the money that I would get for the little calves they would bear I would buy water buffaloes. With the offspring of the buffaloes I would buy horses. With what I could get for the colts, I would soon be very, very rich!'

The Brahmin's eyes glittered as he continued to gaze at the wonderful pot of barley meal hanging over his bed. 'Once rich' he went on, 'I would buy myself a large house. I would furnish it magnificently. I would then plan a splendid feast.

'To the feast I would invite the richest man in the city. He would find me so gracious and entertaining that he would want me to marry his daughter, after giving her a rich dowry, of course.

'In due time we would have a son whom I would name Soma-sarman. When my son would be old enough so that I could bounce him on my knee, I would take the boy and –.'

The Brahmin was so carried away by his dream that he flung one leg up to cross the other. His foot struck the clay pot hanging over his head, and smashed it. In a moment he was covered with white meal from head to foot. Not only was his dream spoiled, but his precious barley meal as well.

'He who spends wealth before he has it is like the Brahmin and the barley meal'.

[32]

Partly for fun, partly for practical purposes, and partly to astonish the natives, I learnt to count to ten in Hindi. The word for five is 'panch', pronounced 'punch'. When we mix punch, we are using the Hindi word, for punch traditionally contains wine, water, lemon, sugar and spices – five ingredients.

The legendary book from which *The Brahmin's Tale* comes is believed originally to have contained twelve volumes, seven of which were lost leaving us with those five known as The Panchatranta.

It would undoubtedly have found its way, either officially or unofficially into the childhood of even so grand a person as . . . Muzaffer Khan, son to the Nawab of Cambay.

In *Lives of the Indian Princes*, by C. H. Allen, (1984), he writes . . .

My education was mainly in the hands of four people. There was an Irish lady who taught me English, a master who taught me almost every other subject, the Mullah who taught me The Koran, and the Hindu Kaviraj, or court poet. So by the time I was six or seven the English side, the Islamic side and the Hindu side were all taken care of. As well as teaching the Koran the Mullah also taught Urdu, Hindi and Arabic, and in the process would tell us tales that were part of Islamic lore. The Kaviraj had his own property six or seven miles from Palanpur city, but he lived in the palace day and night. He was very articulate with a great sense of humour, and the Mahabharat was his favourite subject. He frequently quoted from it, and knew entire passages off by heart. I'd have him for an hour during the day, and again between dinner and going to bed – for story time as it were.

from Book One of *The Mahabharata* (*c.* 500 BC)
[The Tournament]

THE ADVENT OF ARJUN

Gauntleted and jewel-girdled, with his bow of ample height,
Archer Arjun pious-hearted to the gods performed a rite,

Then he stepped forth proud and stately in his golden mail
    encased,
Like the sunlit cloud of evening with the golden rainbow graced,

And a gladness stirred the people all around the listed plain,
Voice of drum, and blare of trumpet rose with sankha's festive
    strain.

'Mark! the gallant son of Pandu, whom the happy Pritha bore,
Mark! the heir of Indra's valour, matchless in his arms and lore,

'Mark! the warrior young and valiant, peerless in his skill of
    arms,
Mark! the prince of stainless virtue, decked with grace and
    varied charms!'

Pritha heard such grateful voices borne aloft unto the sky,
Milk of love suffused her bosom, tear of joy was in her eye!

And where rested Kuru's monarch, joyous accents struck his
    ear,
And he turned to wise Vidura, seeking for the cause to hear:

'Wherefore like the voice of ocean when the tempest winds
    prevail,
Rise the voices of the people and the spacious skies assail?'

Answered him the wise Vidura 'It is Pritha's gallant boy,
Godlike moves in golden armour, and the people shout for joy!'

'Pleased am I,' so spake the monarch, 'and I bless my happy fate,
Pritha's sons like the fires of yajna sanctify this mighty State!'

Now the voices of the people died away and all was still,
Arjun to his proud preceptor showed his might and matchless
   skill.

Towering high or lowly bending on the turf or on his car,
With his bow and glist'ning arrows, Arjun waged the mimic war,

Targets on the wide arena, mighty tough or wondrous small,
With his arrows still unfailing, Arjun pierced them one and all!

Wild-boar shaped in plates of iron coursed the wide-extending
   field,
In its jaws five glist'ning arrows sent the archer wondrous-
skilled,

Cow-horn by a thread suspended was by winds unceasing
   swayed,
One-and-twenty well-aimed arrows on this moving mark he
   laid,

And with equal skill his rapier did the godlike Arjun wield,
Whirling round the mace of battle ranged the spacious tourney
   field!

from *Plain Tales of the Raj* by C. H. Allen (1977)

Young English babes in arms and children must have caught the
flavour of India before they reached the age at which exposure to
the country was deemed unwise, and their parents sent them back
home to school. However, for the *chota sahib* (the little master),
those early years must have been charmed, magical . . .

[35]

The figure of the native nurse, the ayah, dominated the nursery, usually in sari and blouse, and covered in nose-rings, with bangles on her wrists and ankles; when she was moving, you could hear her a mile off.

One of the most charming things I have ever seen was the ayah squatting down on her haunches with a little child saying their rhymes together. Most of them they had translated into a curious kind of Anglo-Indian patois. There was –

Pussy-cat, pussy-cat, where have you been?
I've come out from under the ranee's chair.

I grew up in bright sunshine. I grew up with tremendous space. I grew up with excitement. I grew up believing that white people were superior.

My name is George Nathaniel Curzon,
I am a most superior person.
My cheek is pink, my hair is sleek,
I dine at Blenheim once a week.
George Curzon
Viceroy of India, 1899–1905

We and They by Rudyard Kipling (1919–26)

Father Mother and Me,
Sister and Auntie say
All the people like us are We
And everyone else is They.
And They live over the sea,
While We live over the way,
But – would you believe it? – They look upon We
As only a sort of They!

[36]

We eat pork and beef
With cow horn handled knives.
They who gobble Their rice off a leaf,
Are horrified out of Their lives;
And They who live up a tree,
And feast on grubs and clay,
(Isn't it scandalous?) look upon We
As a simply disgusting They!

We shoot birds with a gun.
They stick lions with spears.
Their full dress is un-
We dress up to Our ears.
They like Their friends for tea,
We like Our friends to stay.
And, after all that, They look upon We
As an utterly ignorant They!

We eat kitcheny food,
We have doors that latch.
They drink milk and blood,
Under an open thatch.
We have Doctors to fee.
They have Wizards to pay.
And (impudent heathen!) they look upon We
As a quite impossible They!

All good people agree,
And all good people say,
All nice people, like Us, are We
And everyone else is They:
But if you cross over the sea,
Instead of over the way
You may end by (think of it!) looking on We
As only a sort of They!

[37]

Night of the Scorpion by Nissim Ezekiel (1965)

I remember the night my mother
was stung by a scorpion. Ten hours
of steady rain had driven him
to crawl beneath a sack of rice.
Parting with his poison – flash
of diabolic tail in the dark room –
he risked the rain again.
The peasants came like swarms of flies
and buzzed the Name of God a hundred times
to paralyse the Evil One.
With candles and with lanterns
throwing giant scorpion shadows
on the sun-baked walls
they searched for him: he was not found.
They clicked their tongues.
With every movement that the scorpion made
his poison moved in Mother's blood, they said.
May he sit still, they said.
May the sins of your previous birth
be burned away tonight, they said.
May your suffering decrease
the misfortunes of your next birth, they said.
May the sum of evil
balanced in this unreal world
against the sum of good
become diminished by your pain.
May the poison purify your flesh
of desire, and your spirit of ambition,
they said, and they sat around

[38]

on the floor with my mother in the centre,
the peace of understanding on each face.
More candles, more lanterns, more neighbours,
more insects, and the endless rain.
My mother twisted through and through
groaning on a mat.
My father, sceptic, rationalist,
trying every curse and blessing,
powder, mixture, herb and hybrid.
He even poured a little paraffin
upon the bitten toe and put a match to it.
I watched the flame feeding on my mother.
I watched the holy man perform his rites
to tame the poison with an incantation.
After twenty hours
it lost its sting.

My mother only said
Thank God the scorpion picked on me
and spared my children.

from *Day of the Scorpion* by Paul Scott (1968)

'Is it true', Sarah asked Aunty Mabel, 'that scorpions kill themselves if you build a ring of fire round them so they know they can't
get out?'

'No', said Aunty Mabel, 'their skins are very sensitive to heat
which is why they live under stones and in holes, and only come
out a lot during the wet. If you build a ring of fire round them,
they're killed by the heat. They look as if they sting themselves to

death because of the way they arch their tails over their bodies, but it is only a reflex action. They're attacking the fire and get scorched to death by it.'

After a few minutes Sarah said 'I see'.

She went upstairs to the bedroom and sat in the window seat. She had a pencil and an exercise book and drew a family tree beginning with Grandpapa.

from a letter of Rabindraneth Tagore

Dear Papumani,

When I heard you were shrivelling up in the scorching heat, I sent you a couple of parcels of good quality rain. Let me know if you get them.

Yours
Grandad

Continuities by Arvind Krishna Mehrotra (1976)

1

This is about the green miraculous trees,
And old clocks on stone towers,
And playgrounds full of light
And dark blue uniforms.
At eight I am a Boy Scout and make a tent
By stretching a bedsheet over parallel bars
And a fire by burning rose bushes,
I know half-a-dozen knots and drink

[40]

Tea from enamel mugs.
I wear khaki drill shorts, note down
The number-plates of cars,
Make a perfect about-turn, for the first time.
In September I collect my cousins' books
And find out the dates of the six Mughals
To secretly write the history of India.
I see Napoleon crossing the Alps
On a white horse.

2

My first watch is a fat and silver Omega
Grandfather won in a race fifty-nine years ago;
It never works, and I've to
Push its hands every few minutes
To get a clearer picture of time.
Somewhere I've kept my autograph-book,
The tincture of iodine in homeopathy bottles,
Bright postcards he sent from
Bad Ems, Germany.
At seven-thirty we are sent home
From the Cosmopolitan Club,
My father says, 'No-bid',
My mother forgets her hand
In a deck of cards.
I sit on the railing till midnight,
Above a worn sign
That advertises a dentist.

3

I go to sleep after I hear him
Snore like the school bell;
I'm standing alone in a back alley
And a face I can never recollect is removing
The hubcaps from our dull brown Ford.

[41]

The first words I mumble are the names of roads,
Thornhill, Hastings, Lytton.
We live in a small cottage,
I grow up on a guava tree
Wondering where the servants vanish
After dinner; at the magic of the bearded tailor
Who can change the shape of my ancestors.
I bend down from the swaying bridge
And pick up the river
Which once tried to hide me:
The dance of the torn skin
Is for much later.

With this rather ominous image, and its wary eye to the future, I want to remind you of Dinesh Sharma. I arranged to meet him one Saturday morning by Hathi Pole – a cross between a clock-tower and a totem-pole, near the centre of Udaipur.

Together we biked to his 'special school'. It turned out to be an art school. The three or four painters sat cross-legged on the floor working on squares of silk and cotton gummed on to sheets of hardboard, copying old paintings, drawing their outlines and filling them in. It was less of an art school than a painting factory for the tourist trade, but Dinesh, although he was still at school, was a part-time student there. It was an indication of how 'fly' he was, that he should already have invested time and energy in the future and had decided on a job – he was going to be a painter. This was no creative calling, for neither Dinesh nor his teacher saw him as an artist: he was a workman, a copier. There was one boy at the school who had 'genius' as the teacher put it, but I was not allowed to see him paint.

One day Dinesh asked me about my family. I told him I had a wife who did the same job as myself, and a little boy of five. He said he would do him a painting of an elephant. As time went by, and our weeks in Udaipur drew to a close, I gently hinted to Dinesh that we would be leaving soon and that I would love to have the painting as a memory. I do not know quite why I was so upset by not receiving the promised painting, but in this one respect, Dinesh really disappointed me. However, it seems typical of him that although I was unable to return to Udaipur myself, I had not heard the last of Dinesh Sharma. He reappears later, in the most extraordinary way.

Although he was the size of a nine year old, Dinesh swore blind he was sixteen. I did not believe him, but if he was telling the truth, this boy, whom my memory holds fixed in childhood, is now a twenty year old, a man.

Early Images

I'm in love with the country and would sooner write about her than anything else . . . I shall find heat and smells and oils and spices, and puffs of temple incense, and sweat and darkness, and dirt and lust and cruelty, and above all, things wonderful and fascinating innumerable.

Kipling

from the diary . . .

I flew to India in January, 1982, leaving England in the grips of a freeze, and looking forward to the warm flannel of air that would embrace me as I stepped from the plane in Delhi in the small hours of the morning. In the event it was drizzling, foggy and cold. In addition, Mr Mukerjee of Mercury Travel was not waiting for me; and to complicate matters still further, I did not know which hotel to contact.

Delhi airport at 1.00 a.m. had the tangy odour of a gymnasium, and the look of a doss-house at rush-hour. People with blankets drawn over their heads were asleep everywhere. Around them ran porters, over them stepped passengers; above their prostrate oblivion people called, whistled and shouted.

I decided to dispose of my luggage before ringing hotels in search of a place to spend the rest of the night.

'Left-luggage' was a well-concealed poky little hole, badly lit with one candle, by whose light the unwilling attendant, swathed in a holey blanket and filthy white rag turban, began filling in forms. He sealing-waxed one to my case, spiked the second, gave me the third, and disappeared into the gloom with all my worldly possessions, and the candle.

I could not find a telephone that worked, but eventually enlisted the help of a couple of security lads whom I caught playing cards in a back room: they let me use their phone. I rang every major hotel in Delhi, and a few besides, but could find no reservation. Frustratingly, I could get no reply from the Oberoi Hotel, which is where I felt sure I was to stay. I could not ring our unit manager who was already filming in the heart of Rajasthan because it would take three hours to book a call, so I headed for the airport hotel with my case, which, to my astonishment, a different attendant, wearing what looked like the same blanket and turban, had retrieved for me from the distant depths of 'Left-luggage'.

My thoughts about Mr Mukerjee of Mercury Travel were less

[47]

than charitable as I trudged among the shrouded sleepers. The airport was quieter now, less of a doss-house, more of a morgue.

En route to the hotel I passed a public telephone, and rang the Oberoi one more time. By this time I knew the number by heart. The phone was answered!

'Hallo. My name is Pigott-Smith of Granada Television. Do you have a reservation for me please?'

'Could you wait, sir?'

Wait. Hope.

'Sorry, Mr Smith. We have no reservation.'

'Did you look under 'P' for Pigott?'

'Could you wait, sir?'

Wait. No hope.

'Hallo . . . Yes. Mr Pigott. We have a reservation. For tomorrow night. If you come now, you can have a room when people leave early for the airport.'

'Thank you. Thank you very much.'

I was too tired to curse them for not answering the phone before. It was 4.00 a.m.

I took a taxi. On the way out of the airport you have to report your name and destination to the authorities. It was alarming, strange. Was there some danger of dacoits? The driver seemed quite friendly – apart from his driving – but then the thuggees had been friendly to their victims; the tired imagination ran riot.

'Good morny, sahib. You first time Delhi?'

I was too worried about the fact that it showed – and the driving – to do more than nod. We drove in the middle of the dark streets. We drove fast. We drove on the wrong side of the road, dodging the ghost-like cows that loomed out of the mist.

At the hotel the driver demanded sixty rupees, but the magnificently-costumed hotel flunky who opened the taxi door advised me that the correct fare was forty rupees. There was some shouting, and a deal was reached. The time was 4.45 a.m.

Since my arrival three long hours ago, I had been introduced to three Indian national games – the telephone, the driving, and

the bartering. I fell into the civilised, Western arms of the
Oberoi Hotel shamefully close to tears.

from *Flowers of Emptiness* by Sally Belfrage (1981)

The first view of urban India is surely the worst in the world. It can
never again be so shocking; one could never again survive the
repetition of its first assault on the senses. The degradation and
the hopeless hordes are so beyond the worst expectations that
there is no armour, no protection possible.

Beside me the driver is barefoot. Perhaps it gives him extra
sensitivity on the pedals for his hair's breadth escapes from
certain doom, which occur about once a block. It is a wonder he
can see, having festooned the car, sun visor to dashboard with
garlands of limp, yesterday's flowers. But blindly or not, he surges
through the competition – a choke of pedestrians and cows, bikes
and motorbikes, horse- and man-drawn carts, buses and many
brightly-painted trucks announcing on their rears HORN OK
PLEASE – advice adhered to universally. Indeed a child might
take the noise for a propellant – we never stop tooting as we
overtake whatever's in the way, blast of outrage in return, multiple
missings-by-an-inch. It is amazing to be so near disaster and to so
barely feel it, because everyone in view is so much nearer a
disaster that is more potent still. How can they be alive? So many
people! When we stop at a red light (the driver turning off the
engine to conserve petrol) they swoop on us crying 'Ma! Ma!
Ma!': the skeletal, the blind, tiny children carrying still tinier
ones, many with the reddish hair of kwashiorko, mutilated stumps
poking through the window, a vast humiliation grown stoic with
need – for when you put a coin in a hand, the hand does not retreat
to make room for another, but instantly returns. You have to keep
the windows shut against them finally or they will not let you drive

[49]

away; then open them quickly for the brief forward sprints or the heat is unendurable.

from *Portrait of India* by Ved Mehta (1970)

On sidewalks and streets, bamboo and burlap lean-to's, prostrate bodies with bundles, sacred bulls chewing on husks of coconut. Smells – dung, urine, sweat, incense, jasmine. Women scooping up and patting cow-dung, and other women cooking on fires of cow-dung chips. Heat at 117 degrees. Children washing in runnels.

Roadside stalls. Signboards: 'Four Annas shave, Eight Annas Headcut, Ten Annas Singeing Ladies' Heads.' 'Loafer's Delight Restaurant. Mutton Cutlis Our Specialty. Eat Them, Enjoy Them, Repeat Them.' Pan-wallahs folding individual scented betel leaves stuffed with lime, catechu, betelnuts. Icemen. Sherbet-wallahs – cool blends of fruit juices, served in gaudy glasses. Fortune-tellers and astrologers. More hawkers and venders, with coconut meat and coconut milk, coir intoxicants and arrack, lotus flowers.

Other aromas: freshly ground pomegranite seed, coriander seed, cumin seed, mustard seed; mint, ginger, cardamon, turmeric, cinnamon, cloves, bayleaf; ghi, chilies, peppers, chutneys. Narrow, cobbled streets, and more stalls, more kiosks, more bazaars. A bookseller and publisher, a goldsmith, a butcher shop with goats being driven through the door. Everywhere: 'Baksheesh! Baksheesh! Baksheesh!'

A twentieth century poem on poverty

POVERTY POEM   by Nissim Ezekiel

She paused when the coffee came,
thanked the waiter, and said:
'I passed him by, of course,
poor child, he held my eyes,
sitting still, almost naked,
small and slightly bent, alone.'

We sipped the coffee, found it good.

'Before he released me,
he smiled and I smiled back,
I turned and gave him a coin,
past belief in that or anything.'

She didn't know beggars in India
smile only at white foreigners.

'Indians are a friendly people, anyway,'
she said. 'So they are,' I agree,
'so they are.' She stares at me
dubiously. I listen to the buzzing air.

Perhaps she thinks it best
not to argue. I think so too.

A second century poem on poverty
from the *Panchatranta*

A beggar to the grave-yard hied
And there 'Friend corpse, arise,' he cried;
'One moment lift my heavy weight
Of poverty; for I of late
Grow weary, and desire instead
Your comfort; you are good and dead.'
The corpse was silent. He was sure
'Twas better to be dead than poor.

from *Exile* by R. Parthasarathy (1977)

The city reels under the heavy load
of smoke. Its rickety legs break
wind, pneumatically, of course,

in the press of traffic.
The sun burns to cigarette ash.
Clouds hiccough, burp

from too much fume. Birds, too,
struggle, pressing thin feathers
against the glass of air.

I am through with the city.
No better than ghettos, the suburbs.
There, language is a noise,

and streets unwind like cobras
from a basket. A cow stands
in the middle combing the traffic.

A cloud unfurls, scarves in the evening.
I loosen the knot in my throat,
and set off towards the sea.

The last sun comes hurtling at me.
Sand turns gold in my hand.
Boats squiggle on the water.

Cautiously, masts sniff at the wind,
wipe off the odour
of land with clean sails.

from *Portrait of India* by Ved Mehta (1970)

In my head, images of Calcutta surface like suppressed night-
mares rising to haunt the conscious mind. A leprous beggar drags
himself through a crowded Calcutta bazaar; his face is ulcerated,
his hands are mutilated, and his lungs and vocal cords are so
damaged that his plea for alms is little more than a croaking sob;
the people, themselves thin and sickly-looking, shrink back to
make way for him, their faces showing the dread of contagion. If
there were any consolation in the belief commonly held among
the well-off that since Calcutta's poor live like animals their pain
is less than human, the crying leper destroys that belief and leaves
me with no consolation whatever.

from the diary . . .

Even after four months in India, I would on occasion be quite unable to cope with it. Days of feeling at home would end suddenly when the alienness pierced my defences . . . a leper's mutilated hand poking through the taxi window pleading for baksheesh, a young child running across the street to pick up barehanded a newly deposited load of steaming holy cow-dung to make 'cakes' for the fire, would send me reeling for the hotel to contain my rising nausea.

It is urban India that appals, the city, where the contrast of the luxurious and the desolate have unavoidably to be sampled in one breath.

The countryside exerts different pressures . . .

from *Deccan* by Brian Thompson (1980)

For a long while the train runs due south, and the sun is directly overhead. The shade temperature outside is in the hundreds. All the windows and the doors to the line are jammed wide open, and in the roof of the first-class accommodation a battery of huge fans churns noisily. The seasoned passengers loll, or sleep; but to a European, travelling south in this stunning way is to go towards otherness. It is the direction of yearning, and even of oblivion. Seen from the window, a tawny countryside peels past, sometimes strewn with boulders, sometimes featureless and deserted. The train runs over huge rumpled riverbeds with not a drop of water in them; it ploughs south, unwaveringly, and it takes all your imagination to remember that this plain was once a great prize of politics, a land fought over, laid waste to, and restored, for generation after generation of princes. For only occasionally does a human figure appear – a young girl crouched in the shade of a stunted tree; a man in white walking resolutely out of the horizon down a perfectly straight road; a woman hoeing.

from the diary . . .

The countryside is much less shocking. The beggar with loin-cloth, forked stick and begging-bowl who one does not like to see being shoo'd from the steps of the Taj Hotel in Bombay by a grandly-dressed native porter seems here, by the side of a deserted road, to be at the very worst, no more than a vulnerable part of nature, like a bird or monkey . . . man . . . another animal.

The Mahratta Ghats by Alun Lewis (1944)

The valleys crack and burn, the exhausted plains
Sink their black teeth into the horny veins
Straggling the hill's red thighs, the bleating goats
– Dry bents and bitter thistles in their throats –
Thread the loose rocks by immemorial tracks.
Dark peasants drag the sun upon their backs.

High on the ghat the new turned soil is red,
The sun has ground it to the finest red,
It lies like gold within each horny hand.
Siva has spilt his seed upon this land.

[55]

Will she who burns and withers on the plain
Leave, ere too late, her scraggy herds of pain,
The cow-dung fire and the trembling beasts,
The little wicked gods, the grinning priests,
And climb before a thousand years have fled,
High as the eagle to her mountain bed
Whose soil is fine as flour and blood-red?

But no! She cannot move. Each arid patch
Owns the lean folk who plough and scythe and thatch
Its grudging yield and scratch its stubborn stones.
The small gods suck the marrow from their bones.

Who is it climbs the summit of the road?
Only the beggar bumming his dark load.

Who was it cried to see the falling star?
Only the landless soldier lost in war.

And did a thousand years go by in vain?
And does another thousand start again?

Leaving England in February 1852, passengers on the
steamship Ripon, of the Peninsular and Orient Company's Line
bound for Calcutta, did not reach their destination until 1st
April – nearly two months. For the next author, this slow
journey was only the beginning of a long trek, which then took
him all the way across India towards the North-West Frontier.
(This extract is a compilation of passages from the first three
chapters). . .

from *Forty-One Years in India,*
From Subaltern to Commander-in-Chief
by Field-Marshal Earl Roberts of Kandahar VC, KP, GCB,
GCSI, GCIE

The metalled highway ended at Meerut, and I had to perform the remainder of my journey to Peshawar, a distance of six hundred miles, in a palankin, or doolie.

The manner of travelling was tedious in the extreme. Starting after dinner, the victim was carried throughout the night by eight men, divided into reliefs of four. The whole of the eight were changed at stages averaging from ten to twelve miles apart. The baggage was also carried by coolies, who kept up an incessant chatter, and the procession was lighted on its way by a torch-bearer, whose torch consisted of bits of rag tied round the end of a stick, upon which he continually poured the most malodorous of oils. If the palankin-bearers were very good, they shuffled along at the rate of about three miles an hour, and if there were no delays, forty or forty-five miles could be accomplished before it became necessary to seek shelter from the sun, in one of the dak-bungalows, or rest-houses erected by Government at convenient intervals along the principal routes. In these bungalows, a bath could be obtained, and sorely it was needed after a journey of thirteen or fourteen hours at a level of only a few inches above an exceedingly dusty road. Even the longest journey must come to an end at last, and early in November I reached Peshawar.

The cantonment of Peshawar had been laid out by Sir Colin Campbell (afterwards Lord Clyde), who commanded there when we first occupied that place in 1849. He crowded the troops, European and Native, into as small a place as possible in order that the station might be the more easily protected from the raids of the Afridis and other robber tribes, who had their homes in the neighbouring mountains and constantly descended into the valley for the sake of plunder. To resist these marauders it was necessary to place guards all round the cantonment. The smaller the

[57]

enclosure, the fewer guards would be required. From this point of view alone was Sir Colin's action excusable, but the result of this overcrowding was what it always is, especially in a tropical climate like that of India, and for long years Peshawar was a name of terror to the English soldier from its proverbial unhealthiness. The water-supply for the first twenty-five years of our occupation was extremely bad, and sanitary arrangements, particularly as regards Natives, were apparently considered unnecessary.

No one was allowed to venture beyond the line of sentries when the sun had set, and even in broad daylight it was not considered safe to go any distance from the station.

From all this, my readers may think that Peshawar, as I first knew it, was not a desirable place of residence; but I was very happy there. There was a good deal of excitement and adventure; I made many friends; and above all, I had, to me, the novel pleasure of being with my father.

The change to the delightful freshness of a Himalayan climate after the Turkish-bath-like atmosphere of the plains in September was most grateful.

from *A Journey in Ladakh* by Andrew Harvey (1983)

Nothing I had read or imagined prepared me for the splendour and majesty of the mountains that first day; that was the first gift Ladakh gave me, a silence before that phantasmagoria of stone, those vast wind-palaces of red and ochre and purple rock, those rock-faces the wind had worked over thousands of years into shapes so unexpected and fantastical the eye could hardly believe them, a silence so truely stunned and wondering that words of description emerge from it very slowly, and at first only in broken images – a river glimpsed there a thousand feet below the road, its waters sparkling in the shifting storm-light, the path below on the bare rocky surface moving with sheep whose wool glittered in the sunlight, small flowers nodding in the crevices of those vast rocks that lined the road, rocks tortured in as many thousand ways as the mountains they are torn from, sudden glimpses of ravines pierced and shattered by the light that broke down from the mountains, of the far peaks of the mountains themselves, secreted in shadow, or illumined suddenly, blindingly, by passing winds of light. And there is no reason in the images, no demure and easily negotiable order, because they emerge from a silence and a wonder so full that they each seem to exist in a time of their own, in a silence of their own, remote from all thought, glimpsed purely as they are, as they are in their essence, in some final purity words do not reach.

Gods and Gurus

The word occurs frequently in the Rig Veda, as a propitiatory epithet applied to the storm-god Rudra, who is implored to look upon his suppliants with compassion, and neither hide the sunlight from them nor be angered should they extol him inadequately. Rudra was evidently regarded as a fierce divinity who ravaged the countryside without discrimination but who also brought rain, without which the crops failed and the people starved. It was therefore natural that Rudra should be addressed with placatory epithets meaning auspicious, propitious, gracious, benign, in the hope of allaying his violent activities.

By the second century BC, the epithet Siva had acquired a separate identity. Representations of Siva holding a trident appear on coins. He is depicted either with two or four arms, and accompanied by his bull-mount, Nandin, but in later periods, the phallus (linga) as well as the trident and the bull are sculpturally represented.

from the diary . . .

The boat trip from India Gate, Bombay harbour to Elephanta was to last an hour.

A small green hump of island grew into focus through the steam of the harbour. A man asleep in a small boat had a fishing-line wound round his toe. Cows mooched on the beach. A long climb up the steps towards the shrine, led past the inevitable tourist bric-a-brac to the caves, whose entrance stood at the top of a rocky hill.

The caves are man-made, hewn out of the rock over 5,000 years ago. 'Caves' is misrepresentative, because they are large and fairly light. No possibility of Miss Quested being assaulted in here: you can see daylight from anywhere within the sculpted chambers. On the walls all around are the carvings which are an integral part of the hill, into which the caves are set. These bas-reliefs are devoted to Lord Siva, to Parvati his consort, and other less-known and more confusing contortions of Hindu mythology. They are impressive but unaffecting.

At the back of the caves, and only dimly discernable at first, but becoming clearer as you focus on its massiveness, is an astonishing and breathtaking monument – the carved stone head of Siva Himself, standing in, and part of, an enormous recess deep in the bowels of the hill out of which it has been carved. It is probably forty feet high. It is not only the scale of the achievement, but the massive, infinite stillness of the face which is awe-inspiring. The head, however, still as it is, holds a secret, and reveals itself gently, but powerfully. It is a 'triple head'. Slowly, through the gloom, you discover on either side of the face, and growing like ears as it were, a right and left profile. Siva looks at you, and into you. You can only return his look but He, at the same time, is looking elsewhere. This is Siva, the eternal ruler, looking before and after, the all-seeing, overpowering you with an omniscience that makes you acutely aware of your own minute mortality.

from *Meditations of a Hindu Prince* by A. C. Lyall (1889)

Here, in this mystical India, the deities hover and swarm
Like the wild bees heard in the tree-tops, or the gusts of a
    gathering storm;
In the air men hear their voices, their feet on the rocks are seen,
Yet we all say, 'Whence is the message, and what may the
    wonders mean?'

A million shrines stand open, and ever the censer swings,
As they bow to a mystic symbol, or the figures of ancient kings;

[64]

And the incense rises ever, and rises the endless cry
Of those who are heavy laden, and of cowards, loth to die.

For the Destiny drives us together, like deer in a pass of the
    hills,
Above is the sky, and around us the sound of the shot that kills;
Pushed by a Power we see not, and struck by a hand unknown,
We pray to the trees for shelter, and press our lips to a stone.

The trees wave a shadowy answer, and the rock frowns hollow
    and grim,
And the form and the nod of the demon are caught in the
    twilight dim;
And we look to the sunlight falling afar on the mountain crest,
Is there never a path runs upward to a refuge there and a rest?

BRAHMA

Brahma is represented as the Creator in late Vedic works. He
became the equilibrium between the two opposing principles
represented by Visnu and Siva respectively, the former
representing preservation and renewal, the latter, elimination
and destruction. In the triad, Brahma, Visnu and Siva constitute
in one form the three aspects of brahman.

In one myth designed to reinterpret allegorically the early
Vedic views, Brahma assumes androgynous form, from which
man and woman were created.

from *A Visit to a Ghani, 1920* by Edward Carpenter

The course of preparation for *gnanam* is called *yogam*, and the person who is going through this stage is called a *yogi* – from the root *yog*, to join – one who is seeking union with the universal spirit. Yogis are common all over India, and exist among all classes and in various forms. Some emaciate themselves and torture their bodies, others seek only control over their minds, some retire into the jungles and mountains, others frequent the cities and exhibit themselves in the crowded fairs, others again carry on the avocations of daily life with but little change of outward habit. Some are humbugs, led on by vanity or greed of gain (for to give to a holy man is highly meritorious); others are genuine students or philosophers; some are profoundly imbued with the religious sense; others by mere distaste for the world. The majority probably take to a wandering life of the body, some become wandering in mind; a great many attain to phases of clairvoyance and abnormal power of some kind or other, and a very few become Adepts of a high order.

In these extracts from William Ayot's play *Bengal Lancer*, which I commissioned from the book by Francis Yeats-Brown, Francis goes to the holy Hindu city of Benares, to find a guru. The speaker is Francis himself, known as 'Y-B'.

There is no sight more harmonious than the Ganges on a bright clear morning with a hundred thousand souls at prayer. There's always a multitude; old and young, but no superstition, no squalor. Just people who wish to glory in simple sunlight and water. The worshipper first offers flowers, rinses his mouth, then kisses the earth. Entering the river, he worships the points of the compass, raising his hands and letting them drip water three times. He then whispers the Gayatri, the oldest prayer known to man – five thousand years old some say. He immerses himself completely, rinses his loincloth and returns to the river steps.

(Y-B is taken by a young girl, Hastini, to the guru, whom he finds sitting by a pier, 'naked, save for a loincloth, and the sacred thread of the twice-born').

GURU: Ah, Francis. I was expecting you, and here you are. How did I know you were coming? That is a long story, and no doubt, being English, you are in a hurry. I knew. I understand you wish to become a yogi. It is written that the sweetness of molasses can only be realised by the tongue, it can never be explained. So it is with yoga. There. Isn't that clever? I got it from one of your English magazines. It is also written that the healing of a sundered soul is a miracle. So what can I tell you? We teach through six principles. We study the individual as composed of five qualities. We study the sound emanating from three places. We pray, we purify, and so the student rises up, up into samadhi.

Y-B: Guru-ji, could I bring my dog?

GURU: Chut, chut, Francis, listen. You eat meat. You indulge in abnormal amounts of exercise. For you the way will be long. Great forces are astir in the world, and you are a part of them. Though your feet have led you to the path, you must live out your time as a soldier. Yes you must. You have come thus far, and you will come again. No, do not be concerned. I shall be sitting under my umbrella for some years yet.

Y-B: When I left, the river was hung with evening mist. Hastini was standing by the pier, looking down the river. I asked her why the guru had sent me away. She said that when I was ready, he could teach me more in five minutes than she could teach in five years. But only then. She observed that it must be stifling always to wear an English mask. Silence fell between us. 'One

[67]

does not fall in love', she said . . . 'one rises into it'. I didn't understand.

THE GAYATRI

OM TAT SAVITUR VARENYAM BHARGO
DEVASYA DIMOHI DHIYO YO NAH PRACHODAYAT OM

Let us contemplate that glorious Light of the divine Savitur:
     may He inspire our minds.

Francis Yeats-Brown takes this to mean:

O face of the True Sun, now hidden by a disc of gold,
     may we know Thy Reality, and do our whole duty
          on our way to Thy Light.

HANUMAN

It means 'heavy-jawed'. A monkey-chief, and the mythical leader of a large troop of ape-like creatures, whose exploits are related in the Ramayana.

In Northern India he presides over every settlement, the setting-up of his image being a sign of its establishment. Popularly regarded as the patron of wandering acrobats and wrestlers, Hanuman is also noted for his great asceticism, learning and as the 'ninth author of grammar'. In southern India his image often forms part of bells or lamps. In one temple, a sacred tank is dedicated to him where sacrifices are performed by those wishing to have a son.

from *Pax Britannica* by James Morris (1979)

Sometimes the English children of Simla crept up the hill of Jakko, high above the town, to the temple of Hanuman, the monkey-god: and there beneath a tree, alone among the monkeys, they would see a young Englishman dressed in the yellow robes of a sadhu, with a head-dress made of leopard skin. He was Charles de Russet, son of a well-known local contractor, who had abandoned his family and his faith to become a disciple of the Jakko fakir. For two years he sat there, all alone.

Sometimes an attendant came from the temple, to give him food: and sometimes the children, peering through the brush, would hear the old priest calling his monkey-children by name to their victuals – Ajoo! Ajoo! – And away they would bound, Raja and Kotwal and Budhee and Daroga, helter-skelter through the undergrowth, leaving the Englishman silent and solitary beneath his tree.

Silence by Krishnamurti (1969)

Silence has many qualities. There is the silence between two noises, the silence between two notes and the widening silence in the interval between two thoughts. There is that peculiar, quiet, pervading silence that comes of an evening in the country; there is the silence through which you hear the bark of a dog in the distance or the whistle of a train as it comes up a steep grade; the silence in a house when everybody has gone to sleep, and its peculiar emphasis when you wake up in the middle of the night and listen to an owl hooting in the valley; and there is that silence before the owl's mate answers. There is the silence of an old deserted house, and the silence of a mountain; the silence between two human beings when they have seen the same thing, felt the same thing, and acted.

That night, particularly in that distant valley with the most ancient hills with their peculiar-shaped boulders, the silence was as real as the wall you touched. And you looked out of the window at the brilliant stars. It was not a self-generated silence; it was not that the earth was quiet and the villagers were asleep, but it came from everywhere – from the distant stars, from those dark hills and from your own mind and heart. This silence seemed to cover everything from the tiniest grain of sand in the river-bed – which only knew running water when it rained – to the tall, spreading banyan tree and a slight breeze that was now beginning. There is the silence of the mind which is never touched by any noise, by any thought or by the passing wind of experience. It is this silence that is innocent, and so endless. When there is this silence of the mind action springs from it, and this action does not cause confusion or misery.

The meditation of a mind that is utterly silent is the benediction that man is ever seeking. In this silence every quality of silence is.

from *My Guru and his Disciple* by Christopher Isherwood (1980)

November 12, 1940. Headache this evening, and rheumatism in my hip. So I did my meditation sitting upright on a chair in my room. Perhaps because of the headache, concentration was much easier than usual. My mind soon became calm. Sitting with closed eyes in the darkness, I suddenly 'saw' a strip of carpet, illuminated by an orange light. The carpet was covered with a black pattern, quite unlike anything we have in the house. But I could also 'see' my bed, standing exactly as it really stands. My field of vision wasn't in any way distorted.

As I watched, I 'saw', in the middle of the carpet, a small dirty-white bird, something like a parrot. After a moment, it began to move, with its quick stiff walk, and went under the bed. This wasn't a dream. I was normally conscious, aware of what I saw and anxious to miss no detail of it. As I sat there, I felt all around me a curiously intense silence, like the silence of deep snow. The only sinister thing about the bird was its air of utter aloofness and *intention*. I had caught it going about its business – very definite business – as one glimpses a mouse disappearing into its hole.

November 13. I told the Swami about the parrot, this evening. He said it was a 'symbolic vision', not a hallucination. On the whole, he seemed pleased. He thought it a sign that something is happening to my consciousness. Probably, he said, there will be other visions. I must take no particular notice of them, and not regard them as a matter for self-congratulation. They have no special significance. The psychic world is all around us, full of sub-creatures, earthbound spirits, etc. To be able to see them is just a knack, a minor talent. Dogs see spooks all the time. It is dangerous to let them interest you too much. At best, they are a distraction from the real objectives of the spiritual life. At worst, they may gain power over you and do you harm.

VISNU

'Pervader'. A minor Vedic personification of solar energy, who is described as striding through the seven regions of the universe in seven steps. A member of the Hindu triad, he is the preserver of the universe and the embodiment of goodness and mercy. To Vaisnavas he is the Supreme Being from whom everything emanates.

In Mysore I found myself a guru – a teacher of yoga – which I have studied vaguely over the years. His *nallayam* (workshop) was a fascinating place where there was one American studying hard, but where the Indians used to pop in casually for a spot of yoga on their way to work.

from the diary . . .

I would take an auto-rickshaw to the *nallayam* whenever I had time: sometimes very early, more often at the end of the day's filming. Guru-ji always welcomed me warmly.

'Come, Tim, come. Shooting?'

'Finished for today, Guru-ji.'

'Now you work.'

'No, Guru-ji. You work, I suffer.'

'No pain, Tim, no gain.'

He padded barefoot round the darkening *nallayam* in his loose white cotton loin wrap, leaving me to get on with the *asanas* (postures) that I could cope with, reappearing miraculously for the ones I found troublesome – he knew what they would be. His scalp was completely hairless, shining – dark oak brown. His skin was vibrantly healthy, and his large clear eyes shone in the darkness, his whole being tinged with the reflected glow of the sunset outside. He looked forty: he was sixty-two. He had energy and calm. He also had a bit of a tummy

[72]

which surprised me, and he never seemed to perform the *asanas* himself, – claiming to have 'lost his powers' – although the pictures on the walls were ample evidence of his skill. One day I asked him how many different types of headstand there were, and he said, 'I show. Headstand – seven types. See.' And he did them all, one after the other.

He spent some time every day with a crippled young American girl, and was beginning to restore life slowly to her thin and lifeless legs, but another girl was leaving the *nallayam* because she said Guru-ji had a sexual problem, and touched her up whilst 'helping' her. Saint or sinner, he was certainly enigmatic.

One day I learned from one of the others at the *nallayam* that Guru-ji had 'lost his powers' because of his son. During Guru-ji's long absences establishing a *nallayam* in San Diego, his son had been left in charge in Mysore. Guru-ji had been very angry to discover on his return that his son had not run things the way he would have wished: they had a violent and angry confrontation, as a result of which Guru-ji's son had tragically committed suicide.

My short time in the *nallayam* has given me an increased knowledge of yoga which is valuable, and a demysticised attitude to it which is invaluable, and it has left me with a sneaking desire to return: to know this remarkable and hypnotic man better, and to take myself a little further along the path of yoga. As they say in India, of the man who has seen the potential of spiritual power –

'He who has been bitten by the cobra, will surely die.'

GANESA

The elephant-headed god of wisdom is described as a demon who possesses men and women and hinders them, but when propitiated and praised, assists them.

In modern times he is regarded as the personification of those qualities which overcome difficulties, the typical embodiment of success in life, and its accompaniments of good-living, peace and prosperity.

As an explanation of Ganesa's solitary tusk, it is related that the moon and the twenty-seven asterisms laughed at him when his belly had burst open and released a large number of cakes which he had eaten. In his rage, he broke off one of his tusks and threw it at the moon which gradually became dark.

from *Bengal Lancer* by Francis Yeats-Brown (1930)

'You Englishmen are practical about material things. Be practical about mysticism also. Build your Rome brick by brick.'

'I have no straw for the bricks of my mind Pandit-ji.'

'When you are ready to build, Hazoor, you will find the straw. It always happens so.'

Women

from the diary . . .

Whenever I met the Indian actors of the cast, and was lost for words, we could easily get to know each other by talking about the large chunks of Urdu that I had to speak in the film. I ended up with as many different ways of saying any one word as there are actors or dialects in India. One such occasion sticks in my mind for two reasons.

The lady in question was the diminutive and utterly delightful Kamini Kaushal, who plays Aunt Shalini so touchingly. In her day she had been a big star of Hindi films, and her acting was premeditated in the style of the Indian dance: for any one moment there was a dictionary of suitable looks or gestures which would have been permissible. Talking to her about the language, she mentioned its phonetic simplicity. 'It looks as it sounds' she said.

I'm not sure this is true, but Khamini then proceeded to tell me a little story which led her into a mistake of pronunciation which was very droll and very charming.

She told me that she frequently had to compère awards ceremonies in India, and that in order be able to pronounce their names correctly, she always asked the finalists to write them out phonetically.

'That way' she smiled confidently, 'I never make mistakes, with the consonants, or the wobels.'

The other reason that I remember Khamini so well, is that apart from her and Zohra Segal – who is such fun as Aunt Lily in the early episodes – I did not meet many Indian women. The few that I did encounter were intelligent career women of a certain class, fabulously, expensively dressed, confident, high-powered and devastatingly almost self-consciously charming. It was difficult to meet the notional 'average' woman. Women generally seemed to be treated differently; almost as if the notion of 'purdah' was operating on a national scale.

[77]

There was a time when I conceived this entire anthology in the shape of 'the life of a woman', because, ironically, I came across so much literature about women in India. In addition, the huge distance between the native Indian women, and the English memsahibs who swept imperially into their midst, gave pause for thought.

In the event, I have chosen to illustrate this area of contrast simply by alternating between English and Indian extracts; I hope you will draw your own conclusions.

Tribulations of Twashtri from *Indian Stories*
by F. W. Bain (1913–20)

In the beginning, when Twashtri came to the creation of woman, he found that he had exhausted his materials in the making of man, and that no solid elements were left. In this dilemma, after profound meditation, he did as follows. He took the rotundity of the moon, and the curves of the creepers, and the clinging of tendrils, and the trembling of grass, and the slenderness of the reed, and the bloom of flowers, and the lightness of leaves, and the tapering of the elephant's trunk, and the glances of deer, and the clustering of rows of bees, and the joyous gaiety of sunbeams, and the weeping of clouds, and the fickleness of the winds, and the timidity of the hare, and the vanity of the peacock, and the softness of the parrot's bosom, and the hardness of adamant, and the sweetness of honey, and the cruelty of the tiger, and the warm glow of the fire, and the coldness of snow, and the chattering of jays, and the cooing of the kokila, and the hypocrisy of the crane, and the fidelity of the chakrawaka; and compounding all these together he made woman, and gave her to man.

But after one week, man came to him, and said: Lord, this creature that you have given me makes my life miserable. She chatters incessantly, and teases me beyond endurance, never leaving me alone: and she requires incessant attention, and takes all my time up, and cries about nothing, and is always idle; and so I have come to give her back again, as I cannot live with her. So Twashtri said: Very well: and he took her back. Then after another week, man came again to him, and said: Lord, I find that my life is very lonely since I gave you back that creature. I remember how she used to dance and sing to me, and look at me out of the corner of her eye, and play with me, and cling to me; and her laughter was music, and she was beautiful to look at, and soft to touch: so give her back to me again. So Twashtri said: Very well: and gave her back again. Then after only three days, man came back to him again, and said: Lord, I know not how it is; but after all I have come to the conclusion that she is more of a trouble than a pleasure to me: so please take her back again. But Twashtri said: Out on you! Be off! I will have no more of this. You must manage how you can. The man said: But I cannot live with her. And Twashtri replied: Neither could you live without her. And he turned his back on man, and went on with his work.

from *Plain Tales of the Raj* by C. H. Allen (1977)

The standard mode of travel to India was on board the P & O from Tilbury or Southampton to Bombay. Seasoned travellers had their passages booked on the Port side of the ship going Out and Starboard Home, travelling POSH and so avoiding the worst of the sun. The accepted time for 'coming out' was in the autumn. The ship was mainly full of people returning from leave, either civil servants or military or business people and quite a number of young girls going out for the Christmas holidays to stay for two or three months during the Cold Weather with their relations or friends. In those days they were known in India as the Fishing

Fleet. The Fishing Fleet was by long-established custom made up of the 'highly eligible, beautiful daughters of wealthy people living in India. This was the only way in which they could come out under the protection of their parents, to meet eligible young men and marry'. Those who failed returned to England in the spring and were known as the Returned Empties.

Indian Women by Shiv K. Kumar (1976)

In this triple-baked continent
women don't etch angry eyebrows
on mud walls.
   patiently they sit
   like empty pitchers
   on the mouth of the village well
pleating hope in each braid
of their Mississipi-long hair
looking deep into the water's mirror
   for the moisture in their eyes.
   with zodiac doodlings on the sands
   they guard their tattooed thighs
waiting for their men's return
till even the shadows
roll up their contours
   and are gone
   beyond the hills.

I'm going to Bombay by Thomas Hood (1830)

I

My hair is brown, my eyes are blue,
And reckoned rather bright;
I'm shapely, if they tell me true,
And just the proper height;
My skin has been admired in verse,
And called as fair as day –
If I *am* fair, so much the worse,
I'm going to Bombay!

II

At school I passed with some éclat;
I learned my French in France;
De Wint gave lessons how to draw,
And D'Egville how to dance:–
Crevelli taught me how to sing,
And Cramer how to play –
It really is the strangest thing –
I'm going to Bombay!

III

I've been to Bath and Cheltenham Wells,
But not their springs to sip, –
To Ramsgate – not to pick up shells, –
To Brighton – not to dip.
I've toured the Lakes, and scoured the coast
From Scarboro' to Torquay –
But though of time I've made the most,
I'm going to Bombay!

[81]

IV

By Pa and Ma I'm daily told
To marry now's my time,
For though I'm very far from old,
I'm rather in my prime.
They say while we have any sun
We ought to make our hay –
But India has so hot a one,
I'm going to Bombay!

V

My cousin writes from Hyderapot
My only chance to snatch,
And says the climate is so hot,
It's sure to light a match.
She's married to a son of Mars,
With very handsome pay,
And swears I ought to thank my stars
I'm going to Bombay!

VI

She says that I shall much delight
To taste their Indian treats;
But what she likes may turn me quite,
Their strange outlandish meats.
If I can eat rupees, who knows?
Or dine, the Indian way,
On doolies and on bungalows –
I'm going to Bombay!

VII

She says that I shall much enjoy, –
I don't know what she means, –
To take the air and buy some toy,

In my own palankeens, –
I like to drive my pony chair,
Or ride our dapple grey –
But elephants are horses there –
I'm going to Bombay!

VIII

Farewell, farewell, my parents dear
My friends, farewell to them!
And oh, what costs a sadder tear,
Good-by, to Mr M.! –
If I should find an Indian vault,
Or fall a tiger's prey,
Or steep in salt, it's all *his* fault
I'm going to Bombay!

IX

That fine new teak-built ship, the Fox,
A 1 – Commander Bird,
Now lying in the London Docks,
Will sail on May the third;
Apply for passage or for freight
To Nichol, Scott, & Gray –
Pa has applied and sealed my fate –
I'm going to Bombay!

X

My heart is full – my trunks as well;
My mind and caps made up,
My corsets, shaped by Mrs Bell,
Are promised ere I sup;
With boots and shoes, Rivarta's best
And dresses by Ducé,
And a special licence in my chest –
I'm going to Bombay!

[83]

Bhartrhari (*c.* 500 AD)

On sunny days there in the shade
Beneath the trees reclined a maid
Who lifted up her dress (she said)
To keep the moonbeams off her head.

from *Plain Tales of the Raj* by C. H. Allen (1977)

Of all the hill stations of India Simla was by far the most glamorous, so much so that some critics considered it 'not really part of India'. There were a lot of married women and there were very few men – and most of the men were in the secretariat or some sort of office job and were, as a rule, rather sober sorts of characters. On the other hand, the young men who came up for brief periods were on holiday and on the loose.

In the two summers I spent at Simla I never thought about doing anything but amusing myself. It was excessively gay. My record was twenty-six nights dancing running, at the end of which I could hardly keep awake, but I had to attend an official dinner that my mother was giving and was severely reprimanded for falling asleep in the middle when talking to a very woolly old judge. It's difficult to convey how enormously romantic the atmosphere was in Simla, the warm starlit nights and bright, huge moon, those towering hills and mountains stretching away, silence and strange exotic smells. Very often coming home from dances the current boyfriend used to walk by the side of the rickshaw, murmuring sweet nothings and holding hands over the side of the hood, nothing much more than that, but it was very romantic. Everything was intensely romantic – and a lot of people were lonely. There was no harm done. There weren't many scandals.

There were certain hill stations to which colonels of Indian

Army regiments would not allow their subalterns to go on leave.
Poodle-faking stations, they were called. Those who went after
the ladies were known as 'poodle-fakers' and were said to come
down from the Hills 'fighting rearguard actions against the
husbands coming up.'

A Village Girl by Mohan Singh (20th century)

A bundle of grass on her head
She came, her hips swinging
Full like wine pitchers
She, the girl from my village

Pataki and mustard flowers
Like blue and yellow eyes
Peep through the green grass

Long blades of grass
Hang over her eyes
Like green tassels
A net of green dreams
Her face caught in it

She lifts her skirt up to her knees
And holds my arm to cross the Suhan River
Ankle-deep water rises to her knees, to her waist
Her legs disappear beneath the shimmering water,
And her skirt goes up like an upturned umbrella.

The water goes down her thighs, her knees, her ankles,
So does her skirt
'Thank you brother', she says

Like a koel cooing from a mango grove
And leaves my arm and goes away

On the sandhill her footprints
Gleam like a prisoner's chain
She goes up the mound
Tall and slim like a sugar cane
And becomes part of the green tree

She did not look at me
I could not see her face caught in the green net
But I cannot shake off
The dust of her touch.

My Rival by Rudyard Kipling (1885–1912)

I go to concert, party, ball –
    What profit is in these?
I sit alone against the wall
    And strive to look at ease.
The incense that is mine by right
    They burn before Her shrine;
And that's because I'm seventeen
    And she is forty-nine.

I cannot check my girlish blush,
    My colour comes and goes.
I redden to my finger-tips,
    And sometimes to my nose.
But She is white where white should be,
    And red where red should shine.
The blush that flies at seventeen
    Is fixed at forty-nine.

[86]

I wish *I* had her constant cheek:
  I wish that I could sing
All sorts of funny little songs,
  Not quite the proper thing.
I'm very *gauche* and very shy,
  Her jokes aren't in my line;
And, worst of all, I'm seventeen
  While She is forty-nine.

The young men come, the young men go,
  Each pink and white and neat,
She's older than their mothers, but
  They grovel at Her feet.
They walk beside Her *'rickshaw*-wheels –
  None ever walk by mine;
And that's because I'm seventeen
  And She is forty-nine.

She rides with half a dozen men
  (She calls them 'boys' and 'mashes'),
I trot along the Mall alone;
  My prettiest frocks and sashes
Don't help to fill my programme-card,
  And vainly I repine
From ten to two A.M. Ah me!
  Would I were forty-nine.

She calls me 'darling,' 'pet,' and 'dear,'
  And 'sweet retiring maid.'
I'm always at the back, I know –
  She puts me in the shade.
She introduces me to men –
  'Cast' lovers, I opine;
For sixty takes to seventeen,
  Nineteen to forty-nine.

[87]

But even She must older grow
And end Her dancing days,
She can't go on for ever so
At concerts, balls, and plays.
One ray of priceless hope I see
Before my footsteps shine;
Just think, that She'll be eighty-one
When I am forty-nine!

from *the Hill of Devi* by E. M. Forster (1953)

The Dowager Maharani – Tara Raja was her name – had long been known to me as Dewas-Nuisance-Lady No. 1. Widow to the previous ruler she had supported her nephew's elevation to the throne, but once he was there did nothing but vex him. A row about a silver spoon, which she accused her English companion of stealing, shook the court from top to bottom, and there was still greater trouble over the state jewels which she annexed, and was obliged to give up on his marriage. She squabbled with his mother, danced dressed as a man with her maid-servants, similarly dressed, she was unruly and bizarre, and she tried to poison him. I never could accept the poison story – there seemed to me no conceivable motive for the crime.

She was gracious and amiable to me, also homely, and she had that slight air of despair that suits an Indian lady so well, showing no resentment, only the disillusionment with which a well-bred person faces all life. In appearance she was short and dumpy, but there was nothing grotesque about her: her sari was on the sober side, her expression frank and resigned and if she did not talk English perfectly she anyhow expressed herself perfectly in English. As we poured out tea, or she the tea and I the milk, as we offered one another bread and butter, or blew the flies

[88]

off the little cakes, I have never come nearer to banqueting with Catherine de Medici.

from *The Golden Calm*

An English Lady's Life in Moghul Delhi
Reminiscences by Emily, wife to Sir Edward Clive Bailey

In 1835 she left her house in Delhi on a long journey . . .

I have a hazy recollection of the incidents of our long journey to Calcutta. It was made partly by land in palanquins (covered doolies) and partly in boats – 'budgerows' as they were called – covered barges built of wood, painted green and very comfortably furnished and divided into two rooms each – for sleeping and sitting rooms. A separate 'budgerow' was fitted up for kitchen and servants' use – and this small flotilla kept company together and proceeded quietly down the stream of the great rivers, sometimes towed by men walking on the river bank, sometimes rowed by boatmen on board, sometimes sailing with the wind – but always stopping at sundown, moored to the bank of the river with men posted as 'chokidars' or watchmen to take care of the little flotilla during the night.

from *Costumes and Characters of the British Raj*
by Evelyn Battye

A long time ago, the legend ran, the Maharana of Udaipur became enamoured of a beautiful dancing girl who was also (as most were) an acrobat. He agreed to give her all the jewels and land she wanted on one condition: that she would cross over a tightrope from his City Palace to his Lake Palace. She readily agreed. To her a tightrope was a tightrope and it really made no difference whether it was over land or water.

Late one day all was set for this daring act, the acrobat ready to start, the rope stretching from one palace to the other, sagging in the middle. The populace turned out in thousands to watch from the ramparts of the fortress, while the balconies and turrets of the City and Summer Palaces were crammed with courtiers and servants, the zenana ladies pressing their faces to the latticed windows the better to see the spectacle.

An exclusive party of males glided below in the red and green royal barge, many oarsmen wielding the dripping oars. On the high stern rose a tiered ornamental platform where the Maharana lay back on his silken cushions watching the alluring girl gracefully balancing her way towards him, a long pole in her hands, each dainty brown foot placed carefully and surely before the other, her silver anklets gleaming in the lowering sun, the little bells twinkling in the hushed silence.

The Maharana frowned as she progressed. He sat up as it dawned on him that she was going to reach her goal. She was already more than half way across! He would have to give her anything she asked – all those possessions! In a swift movement he drew his curving sword from its velvet scabbard, and standing up to his full height he stepped forward, and, with one lashing swipe, cut the rope. In the deafening quiet that followed, the cries for help from the dancing girl rent the evening air: those watching took their cue from the Maharana, none daring to move.

When she saw the barge turning away, the girl cursed. With her gasping, gulping, dying breath she cursed the despicable Maharana who had broken his word, and laid a curse on direct heirs succeeding for generations to come. The Pichola Lake waters turned crimson in the sunset as the lovely nautch-girl sank

[90]

for the last time, her spreading hair black and ominous upon the waters.

from *An Indian Attachment* by Sarah Lloyd (1984)

Sarah Lloyd went to live in the house of a Sikh friend whom she nicknamed Jungli, in a village in the Punjab.

I had already had more than my fill of being stared at before coming to the village. And I had naively believed that being with Jungli would put an end to it; staying in a rural community, hardly going out, with Jungli there to protect me – to explain to people I didn't like – would, after the initial interest had died down, be a solution to the problem.

It wasn't of course. The phenomenon had its roots in extreme racial prejudice.

'Isn't she beautiful?' people would say. Beautiful because I was white. Had I been black, Chinese, low caste or of tribal origin, I would have been ignored. And Jungli made no attempt to restrain the viewing.

What I wanted was only partially attainable. To be with Jungli, getting to know him through our growing ability to communicate: that I could have. To indulge my nostalgia for English village life fifty years ago, a life arranged not by machines but by nature, where people and animals lived in close contact, where every tool was comprehensible and the earth was held sacrosanct; that, to a lesser extent, I could also have. But to be a part of Jungli's village, living in the style of its inhabitants, absorbing its customs and sharing its labour: that, for the present, was beyond my reach. For as long as I stayed, I was a guest: I remained an outsider.

I liked being in the village. People were less complicated, less competitive, less spoilt by consumerism than most people in the

West; in the absence of the media they occupied their own reality. I was sympathetic to their way of life and disturbed, therefore, that they should find me so peculiar. Their staring alienated, when I was trying to integrate.

The Mistress by Keki Daruwalla (1982)

No one believes me when I say
my mistress is half-caste. Perched
on the genealogical tree somewhere
is a Muslim midwife and a Goan cook.
But she is more mixed than that.
Down the genetic lane, babus
and professors of English
have also made their one-night contributions.

You can make her out the way she speaks;
her consonants bludgeon you;
her argot is rococo, her latest 'slang'
is available in classical dictionaries.
She sounds like a dry sob
stuck in the throat of darkness.

In the mornings her mouth is sour
with dreams which had fermented during the night.
When I sleep by her side
I can almost hear the blister-bubble
grope for a mouth through which to snarl.
My love for her survives from night to night,
even though each time
I have to wrestle with her in bed.

In the streets she is known.
They hiss when she passes.

Despite this she is vain,
flashes her bangles and her tinsel;
wears heels even though her feet
are smeared up to the ankles with henna.

She will not stick to *vindaloo*, but talks
of roasts, pies, pomfrets grilled.
She speaks of contreau and not cashew
arrack which her father once distilled.

No, she is not Anglo-Indian. The Demellos would
bugger me if they got scent of this,
and half my body would turn into a bruise.
She is not Goan, not Syrian Christian.
She is Indian English, the language that I use.

Time and Stone

from the diary . . .

A Rajput is the son of a ruler. Rajasthan – which used to be
known as Rajputana – is the land of the Rajputs, a large state in
the north-west of India. In the Mewar district of Rajasthan there
is a powerful sense of history and a pride in, for example,
Maharanah Pratap's martial bravery in resisting the mughals.
Even the singular title 'maharanah' is special to this part of India
– it means the first of the maharajahs. The self-sacrifice of Rani
Padmini who burnt herself to death to preserve her fidelity from
a besieging army is another popular story. My guide-book puts it
more succinctly: 'The history of Mewar is full of sacrifices,
patriotism, gallantry and whatnot.'

In the north of this desert state the fortress of Jaissalmeer
looks out on unsympathetic countryside, but here, towards the
south, only an hour's plane-ride from Bombay, the land is
gentler and the sandy brown ranges of hills whose vegetation has
been picked clean by the goats, look from the sky, like wrinkles
on a beach. In these foothills of the Arravali mountains, built
around artificially constructed lakes, nestles the city of Udaipur,
– the 'Venice of the East', founded by Maharana Udai Singh in
1559.

The Rajmahal – the palace of the ruler – runs for some 500
yards along the banks of Pichola Lake, and overlooks the Lake
Palace, a guest-house-island marooned in the still waters. Also
known as the City Palace, it is a magnificent white marble and
sandstone building seven or eight stories high – its crowded,
angled colonnades make it difficult to tell precisely – capped
with massive octagonal cupolas. Forty years ago it was a building
in use, a home for many people, a shelter for many animals and
a garage for the only two motor-cars then in the town whose
life-blood it provided.

Now it is a focal point in the town in memory only. Cardboard
cut-outs of the last maharanah to wield power still stare out

[97]

impassively from hotel lobbies and shop windows. He was crippled, and his wheel-chair is to be found in the museum. The museum is in the palace.

I found a haunting picture of this unfortunate cripple – the Maharanah Sir Bhupal Singh Bahadur GCSI, KCIE – sitting in his wheel-chair with a large rifle resting across his shrivelled thighs. At his dead feet lies a magnificent tiger that he has just shot.

There was no direct heir to this throne, which was taken by some to be the fulfilment of an ancient curse, and it passed to another branch of the family to which Narendra Singh belongs. Brother of the current potentate, he is a handsome man in his mid-forties, lithe and strong, with proud, carved aquiline features: I heard it described as a face typical of the Rajasthani nobility. He has dark, gentle eyes and perfect teeth, which turn out to be a replacement for his own, which were thrashed out by an angry horse.

Narendra creates a picture for me of the palace in its heyday: five hundred people working for eight hours until four in the afternoon: five hundred more replacing them for a second eight hour shift, and being replaced themselves by the next five hundred at midnight – each with a specific and personal job. One girl might collect letters for the ranee from the main gate, and return with any reply: that would be the extent of her job. Another might shoo birds from the trees in the magnificent roof-garden. Narendra then describes the fantastical train of horses, camels, elephants and men that wound its way annually from the Rajmahal, up the narrow twisting road to the family's monsoon palace which perches, now crumbling and unused, on a hill outside the town from where the ruler could survey his rainswept kingdom.

Narendra also recalls the gentle, uncrowded family life of childhood summers in the guest-house, the floating palace, now the Lake Palace Hotel. It is hardly surprising that it disturbs him to eat there in a room, which in his view has not so much been converted as debased into a restaurant: a 125 seater dining-room which overlooks the fountains still playing in the tourist-occupied courtyard. The restaurant staff know Narendra, remember him, and therefore treat him with great deference. The very old chef emerges from the kitchen to make *namaste* and ensure that the food has been enjoyed by his prince, and, as well as recognition of Narendra's status, the cook reveals a genuine pleasure in his humble greeting.

Narendra lives outside the town, having some distaste for the bureaucracy of the palace where his brother the maharanah, and his mother, the begum, reside. I suspect Narendra is a modern man, more realistic than others in his family, for although they live in a palace, they have no power. The maharanah is not even a figurehead. He is simply a figure, lost in time.

Time. Much of India seems unaffected by time. The minutes delude you into thinking they tick by more slowly. I had the added sensation that any act – say, galloping my horse with Narendra over the dusty countryside to his lotus lake – receded into the past more slowly; that it was being captured somehow, preserved somewhere. I felt the same to be true of the three hundred years of British rule: that those centuries are still there, the attitudes trapped in time, the actions held in space, a part of India. Not forgotten. Not judged. Just there . . . still there.

from *The Discovery of India* by Jawaharlal Nehru (1946)

There is a stillness and everlastingness about the past; it changes not and has a touch of eternity, like a painted picture or a statue in bronze or marble. Unaffected by the storms and upheavals of the present it maintains its dignity and repose and tempts the troubled spirit and the tortured mind to seek shelter in its vaulted catacombs. There is peace there and security, and one may even sense a spiritual quality.

A Look from Lipika by Rabindraneth Tagore (1941)

As she was stepping into the carriage, she turned back and gave me a last look. In this vast world, where can I keep this tiny thing? Where can I find a corner where hours, minutes, seconds will not trample it with their steps? The twilight into which fade the golden colours of the clouds – will this look also fade into twilight?

If it is scattered among the things of everyday life – how can it preserve itself among the rubbish of daily chatter and life's piled-up sorrows?

That look, like an instantaneous flash, has come to me, over-whelming all else. I will hold it in songs, imprison it in rhythm, and keep it in Beauty's Paradise.

In this world the might of emperors and the wealth of the rich exist only to die one day. But in a tear, is there not immortality to keep it forever alive?

The clearest symbol I know of the way that India somehow contains the past – of something preserved, in the way that Tagore tries to preserve The Look – is in the town of Fatehpur Sikri.

Ralph Fitch, the first English merchant traveller to India, who arrived in 1583, describes his visit to Agra, and Fatehpur Sikri which was built by Akbar the Great in 1571:

from *Purchas his Pilgrims* by Samuel Purchas (1619)

From thence we went to Agra, passing many Rivers, which by reason of the raine were so swollen that we waded and swamme oftentimes for our lives. Agra is a very great Citie and populous, built with stone, having faire and large streets, with a faire River running by it, which falleth into the Gulfe of Bengala. It hath a faire Castle and strong, with a very faire Ditch. Here bee many Moores and Gentiles, the king is called Zelabdim Echebar: the people for the most part call him The great Mogor.

For thence we went for Fatepore, which is the place where the King kept his Court. The King hath in Agra and Fatepore, as they doe credibly report, one thousand Elephants, thirtie thousand horses, one thousand and foure hundred tame Deere, eight hundred concubines: such store of Ounces, Tygres, Buffles, Cockes and Hawkes that is very strange to see.

Agra and Fatepore are two very great Cities, either of them much greater than London, and very populous. Between Agra and Fatepore are twelve miles, and all the way is a Market of victuals and other things, as full as though a man were still in a Towne, and so many people as if a man were in a Market. They have many fine Carts, and many of them carved and gilded with Gold, with two wheeles which bee drawne with two little Bulls, about the bignesse of our great Dogs in England, and they will runne with any Horse, and carry two or three men in one of these Carts: they are covered with Silke or very fine cloth, and bee used here as our Coaches bee in England. Hither is great resort of Merchants from Persia, and out of India, and very much Merchandize of Silke and Cloth, and of precious Stones, both Rubies, Diamants, and Pearles. The King is apparelled in a white Cabie made like a Shirt tyed with strings on one side, and a little cloth on his head, coloured often-times with red and yellow. None come into his house but his Eunuchs which keepe his women. He keepeth a Greate Court.

from *The Great Moghuls* by Bamber Gascoigne (1971)

Fatehpur Sikri is today the world's most perfectly preserved ghost town. India's climate is gentle to stone if not to people, and a modern visitor could well be persuaded that these intricate casket-like buildings, with their elaborately carved stone ornamentation still crisp and unweathered, had been completed only yesterday.

But to call the present Fatehpur Sikri a town or a city, as is usually done, is slightly misleading. What remains in such perfect state is in fact the palace, though its unique arrangement of vast paved areas dotted with free-standing houses, some of them private dwellings and some assembly rooms, suggests more some architect's image of a small Utopian town for a select community of aesthetes.

The real town occupied a large area round the foot of the hill with the palace and great mosque at its summit. Here the courtiers and the vast legions of camp followers – a capital city in these times was still essentially the imperial camp at home – built themselves dwellings of varying degrees of impermanence while Akbar and his thousands of craftsmen were creating their master-piece up the hill.

The feature which most strongly strikes a western visitor about Akbar's buildings and their immediate predecessors is that they appear to be wooden houses made of stone, in that their techniques of construction and ornamentation are precisely those of craftsmen in wood in other countries. The Indian mason quarried doorways, lintels, screens, bannisters, beams and even floorboards from his native sandstone just as the Tudor carpenter cleft them from the oak.

He then carved their exposed surfaces with very fanciful elaboration, and fitted them together for his final building in

[102]

precisely the same manner, except that gravity enabled him to do away with any system of pegs – the mere weight of the stones would hold them in place.

The palace buildings of Fatehpur Sikri consist of nothing but perfectly tailored chunks and slabs of stone resting on each other; indeed the slabs were mostly brought to the site in a finished state, which greatly speeded the work of construction by making it more one of compilation.

from *Hindu Holiday* by J. R. Ackerley (1932)

The Dewan took me with him to see a bridge being built in the neighbourhood, and I remarked on the poor physique of the builders – lean, under-nourished men with little round bellies – and asked what wages they were getting.

'Twopence halfpenny a day', said the Dewan. They had recently mutinied, he said, and had been given a rise. I asked what their wages had been before the rise.

'Twopence a day', said the Dewan.

He remarked, too, that this was a great advance upon the past, for fairly recent statistics showed that the average wage of a labourer in Garha used to be one and a half rupees (two shillings) a month. Chokrapur does even better. No labourer there gets less than fourpence a day.

I asked whether they did not find it a little problematical to live on even fourpence a day, and he said abruptly:

'Not at all! It is exactly twice as much as they require.' A labourer's expenses were twopence a day, he said – two pounds of grain (barley) which cost him a penny-ha'penny, and a ha'porth of vegetables. He could live on this on his present wages and treat himself every now and then, out of his savings, to rice.

For a little time I watched these poor emaciated creatures

[103]

carrying blocks of stone – eight men to each block, which was
suspended on chains from a long pole. The Dewan said that there
were sculptures on the Garha temples showing that the labourers
a thousand years ago had handled the stone in exactly the same
way.

The next poem describes the massive rock-carvings on the
South-Eastern sea-shore by the temple of Mahabilipuram. It
deals with the infinite complexities of the Hindu religion and its
proliferation of deities. These gods and their sculptured forms
are difficult for us to understand, but the poet, looking at the
obscure carvings, writes . . .

> 'But now that we look without trying to learn
> . . . now we can see, if not hear . . .'

You have to do the same with this poem: do not try to
understand, and understanding will come: this form of
instinctive learning which is rather difficult, rather foreign to
me, is fundamental to yogic thought.

Mahabilipuram by Louis MacNeice (1948)

All alone from his dark sanctum the lingam fronts, affronts the
sea,
The world's dead weight of breakers against sapling, bull and
candle
Where worship comes no more,
Yet how should these cowherds and gods continue to dance in
the rock
All the long night along ocean in this lost border between

[104]

That thronging gonging mirage of paddy and toddy and dung
    And this uninhabited shore?

Silent except for the squadrons of water, the dark grim chargers
    launched from Australia,
Dark except for their manes of phosphorus, silent in spite of the
    rockhewn windmill
        That brandishes axe and knife —
The many-handed virgin facing, abasing the Oaf, the Demon;
Dark in spite of the rockhewn radiance of Vishnu and Shiva and
    silent
In spite of the mooing of Krishna's herds; yet in spite of this
    darkness and silence
        Behold what a joy of life —

Which goes with an awe and a horror; the innocence which
    surmounted the guilt
Thirteen centuries back when an artist eyeing this litter of
    granite
        Saw it for waste and took
A header below the rockface, found there already like a ballet of
    fishes
Passing, repassing each other, these shapes of gopi and goblin,
Of elephant, serpent and antelope, saw them and grasped his
    mallet
        And cried with a clear stroke: Look!

And now we look, we to whom mantra and mudra mean little,
And who find in this Hindu world a zone that is ultra-violet
        Balanced by an infra-red,
Austerity and orgy alike being phrased, it seems, in a strange
    dead language
But now that we look without trying to learn and only look in the
    act of leaping

[105]

After the sculptor into the rockface, now we can see, if not hear, those phrases
    To be neither strange nor dead.

Not strange for all their ingrown iconography, not so strange as our own dreams
Because better ordered, these are the dreams we have needed
    Since we forgot how to dance;
This god asleep on the snake is the archetype of the sleep that we lost
When we were born, and these wingless figures that fly
Merely by bending the knee are the earnest of what we aspire to
    Apart from science and chance.

And the largest of all these reliefs, forty foot high by a hundred,
Is large in more senses than one, including both heaven and the animal kingdom
    And a grain of salt as well
For the saint stands always above on one leg fasting
Acquiring power while the smug hypocritical cat beneath him
Stands on his hindlegs too admired by the mice
    Whom the sculptor did not tell.

Nor did he tell the simple and beautiful rustics
Who saved from their doom by Krishna are once more busy and happy
    Absorbed in themselves and Him,
That trapped in this way in the rock their idyl would live to excite
And at once annul the lust and the envy of tourists
Taking them out of themselves and to find themselves in a world
    That has neither rift nor rim:

A monochrome world that has all the indulgence of colour,
A still world whose every harmonic is audible,

[106]

Largesse of spirit and stone;
Created things for once and for all featured in full while for once
    and never
The creator who is destroyer stands at the last point of land
Featureless; in a dark cell, a phallus of granite, as abstract
        As the North Pole; as alone.

But the visitor must move on and the waves assault the temple,
Living granite against dead water, and time with its weathering
    action
        Make phrase and feature blurred;
Still from to-day we know what an avatar is, we have seen
God take shape and dwell among shapes, we have felt
Our ageing limbs respond to those ageless limbs in the rock
        Reliefs. Relief is the word.

The Grove of the Perfect Being by Alan Ross (1973)

Handsome as Shashi Kapoor,
Idol of the Indian cinema, he is perfectly
Turned out – flowered shirt,
Wide belt, white suit, buckle shoes,
Silvery as a fish with chains and bracelets –
And aware of having a way
With him, though not my way.
He is the self-appointed guide
And impresario to 'the Grove
Of the Perfect Being', at one
With the past and the place,
Site among the mangos of the earliest
Of Bhubaneswar's many temples.

[107]

Son of a priest of a priest,
He assumes the right to whatever perks
Are going; he'd rather
It were a cinema or garage,
But there it is. The patter
Has become second nature,
Kalinga and Asoka, Durga
And Hanuman, the Monkey God,
Rajani and Lingaraj,
More boring than chat about torques
And facias, discbrakes or suspension,
But – with luck – good for some baksheesh.
And leaping in front of us,
Brushing aside our mild demurrings,
He swings his transistor, repeating
Parrot-fashion a lengthy rigmarole
As apparently incomprehensible
To himself as to others,
Flashing a smile like a grand piano.

When it is all over
And 'The Golden Age of temple building'
With its *shikharas* and *toranos*,
Jagamohans and *bhogmandirs*,
Has been confused beyond recognition,
He discourses on the Lord Siva
And his lingam, on Parvati
And the *mithuna* couples whose antics
Are obviously more to his own liking.

And at last allowing us
Actually to enter a temple,
With a sly smirk points to elephants
And what he calls 'cocrodiles',
Cobras and hermits and dancing girls,

[108]

Dwarfs and lions. 'In this one
The cocrodile is entering the water,
And in this one the lady
Is being entered from behind,
One of the popular positions
Favourable for penetration.'

He is pleased with his joke,
Slipped as silkily in as only
Long practice can manage,
And he awaits our reaction,
A bit down for a second,
But soon back in top gear,
Drawing our attention
To what scarcely needed it,
Endless friezes of copulation,
Men and women their legs round each other,
Priests and prostitutes,
The holy and the wholly pleasurable.

At Bhubaneswar there is plenty
Of both, and leaving the Bundu Sagar
'The sacred lake' it is possible
To reflect on the sad separateness
Of our Christian culture,
Puritanism the alternative
To exploitation on the crudest
Of levels. Even here
In this mango-grove of temples,
Nothing is allowed to be
What it was, the exchange
Of favours for their own sake,
Two bodies making what they can
Of momentary ecstasies, before
The curtains come down, the showmen appear.

[109]

from the diary . . .

On my last night in Udaipur, I paid a farewell visit to the
Shreejagdeesh Temple: past the waiting tongas with their lean,
patient horses, and lean sleeping drivers, up the steep narrow
temple steps, between the massive carved elephants and into the
small Vishnu shrine for evening prayers.

It was a lackadaisical, interminable affair; people wandering in
and praying for a bit, making pooja, joining in the Jagdeesh
hymn, wandering off. Babes in arms were brought in, children
played, friends chatted. One dhoti'd old man let rip a terrific fart
during the garbled responses. It didn't noticeably affect his
relationship with his god, or even, for that matter, his
fellow-prayers. If there were any rules governing the evening's
proceedings, simultaneous prayer and flatulence did not appear
to contravene them.

This absence of restriction – which I, as a product of a
rule-book civilisation, tend to find unsettling – has, of course, a
positive aspect. It allows a mind to develop, which, in embracing
everything as a manifestation of God, is not disturbed by
contradictions which offend us. Hinduism does not
compartmentalise in the way we do. Everything seems related.

I am not making out a case for farting in church, but I do envy
the simple ease of access to spiritual joy that I witnessed in this
temple. That's why I used to go back there. I was captivated
by the proximity of body and soul, of the natural and the
sophisticated, and I sensed the power of this intriguing
combination.

I think it explained why I was so often – rather unusually for
me – so close to tears in India: it opened me up. It removed the
necessity for habitual, strict self-control, and made the normally

protected emotional areas more available. This very Indian union of the unaffected and the civilised will, I suspect, always elude and therefore always intrigue the English.

Bonds of Friendship

from *The Soul of India* by Amaury de Riencourt (1950)
from Chapter 12 Birth of an Empire: Rise of British Power

Great and enduring empires are the result of circumstances rather than of men's conscious will. They just happen because of historical necessity, because countries fall to pieces owing to internal circumstances and because outsiders are often compelled, often against their own wishes, to pick up the pieces. They endure because of the tacit acquiescence of the conquered and last only so long as this acquiescence lasts. With very few exceptions the Indian populations had long ago lost all interest in politics, leaving warfare to professional soldiers and statesmanship and diplomacy to the Caesarian rulers who fought each other ruthlessly. Mostly self-governing through their caste and village-councils, they accepted more or less meekly the rulers which fate decreed for them, many of whom were low-caste adventurers who were willing to soil their hands in the dirty world of politics. They had accepted for hundreds of years the rule of alien Muslims and, except for sporadic rebellions, had merely tried to tighten the bonds knitting their society together and let the Muslims rule as they pleased. And this attitude did not change when the Europeans appeared on the scene.

That one involvement brings on another and so on ad infinitum, was soon proved by the fact that the British had to extend their sway further and further beyond the frontiers of India proper for the sheer sake of protecting their existing possessions.

From my diary . . .

There was a certain childish innocence about many of the men who wielded power in the early days of the empire. I was told an extraordinary story by one of the Lawrence family, whom we know best through Sir Henry Lawrence, Governor of Lucknow at the time of the Siege. I believe it was Henry's brother who was given the famous Koh-i-nor diamond – one of the largest in the world – by Ranjit Singh, as part of the price for his defeat in the endless Sikh wars in the Punjab. Lawrence put it in his waistcoat pocket where it remained for several weeks. When he was eventually asked about it by Queen Victoria, both he and his servant had some difficulty in remembering, and tracing it. It was eventually discovered and duly despatched to the Tower of London, where it has remained ever since, as part of the Crown Jewels.

from *A Concise History of India* by Francis Watson (1979)

The most fateful decision of Bentinck's term (1828–35) was that which in his last year channelled the official education policy, first sanctioned in 1813, towards 'imparting to the Native population knowledge of English literature and science through the medium of the English language'. Victory over the 'orientalists', who wanted the available funds to be used in continuance of the Warren Hastings policy of patronizing Persian, Arabic and Sanskrit studies, was clinched by Macaulay in the famous Minute which argued that 'a single shelf of a good European library is worth the whole native literature of India and Arabia'. Though his eloquence derived from ignorance of what he was denigrating, his cause answered the modernizing aspirations of the Ram Mohun Roy persuasion, who shared Bentinck's belief in the English language as 'the key to all improvements'. An important step taken at the same time was the replacement of Persian by English as the official language and in the higher law-courts, and by regional languages in the lower courts.

The English Language, ironically presented a unifying aspect: an army officer could be understood by more of his men if he spoke in English than if he were to use any one of the numerous regional dialects. There has always been something particularly delightful about the way that Asians have tried to master the language.

from *No Heaven for Gunga Din*
by Ali Mirdrekvandi Gunga Din, edited by John Hemming

Dear Captain,

I have learnt about 1000 words of English during my working. as I had a good interest to learn English, I have agreed with myself I must be destroyed unless to learn it.

I am out of work and cannot learn English without job. I have come here to pray you to give me a job at a British soldier, perhaps during my service to learn English. You may be sure I am very active for work as soon as a work to be given to me and can achieve it very bravely.

You see that I am durty and have no clothing. I have no fault, because a thief has stolen al my clothings. I am waiting the strength of God get into your heart to make you put me on work.

However there is another point of view, and in *The Jewel in the Crown* it is expressed by the Hindu teacher and revolutionary Pandit Baba, who is appalled by his countrymen's linguistic acquiescence. He upbraids Hari Kumar with the jibe . . . 'Do you not feel shame, always to speak in the language of a foreign power?'

from *Short Walk in the Hindu Kush* by Eric Newby (1984)

Newby is reading . . . *Notes on the Bashgali (Kafir Language)*, by
Colonel J. Davidson of the Indian Staff Corps., 1901. Whilst
Newby is struggling with this fairly heavy fare, his companion is
attempting to divert his mind from the pain in his feet and the
murmurings of his stomach, with the more digestible *Hound of
the Baskervilles.*

Reading the 1,744 sentences with their English equivalents, I
began to form a disturbing impression of the waking life of the
Bashgali Kafirs.

'*Shtal latta wōs bā padrē ū prētt tū nashtontī mrlosh.* Do you know
what that is?'

It was too late to surprise Hugh with a sudden knowledge of the
language.

'What?'

'In Bashgali it's "If you have had diarrhoea many days you will
surely die."'

'That's not much use,' he said. He wanted to get on with Conan
Doyle.

'What about this then? *Bilugh âo na pī bilosh.* It means, "Don't
drink much water; otherwise you won't be able to travel."'

'I want to get on with my book.'

Wishing that Hyde-Clarke had been there to share my felicity I
continued to mouth phrases aloud until Hugh moved away to
another rock, unable to concentrate. Some of the opening gam-
bits the Bashgalis allowed themselves in the conversation game
were quite shattering. *Inī ash ptul p'mich ē manchī mrisht wariā'm.*
'I saw a corpse in a field this morning', and *Tū chi sē biss gur bītī?*
'How long have you had a goitre?', or even *Iā jūk noi bazisnā
prēlom.* 'My girl is a bride.'

Even the most casual remarks let drop by this remarkable
people had the impact of a sledgehammer. *Tū tōtt baglo piltiā.* 'Thy
father fell into the river.' *Ī non angur ai; tū tā duts angur ai.* 'I have

nine fingers; you have ten.' *Or manchī aiyo; buri aīs̲h kutt.* 'A dwarf has come to ask for food.' And *Iā chitt bitto tū jārlom,* 'I have an intention to kill you', to which the reply came pat, *Tū bilug̲h lē bidiwā manchī assis̲h,* 'You are a very kind-hearted man.'

Their country seemed a place where the elements had an almost supernatural fury: *Dum allangitī atsitī ī sundī basnâ brā.* 'A gust of wind came and took away all my clothes', and where nature was implacable and cruel: *Z̲hī marē badist tā wō ayō kakkok damītī gwā.* 'A lammergeier came down from the sky and took off my cock.' Perhaps it was such misfortunes that had made the inhabitants so petulant: *Tū biluk wari walal manchī assis̲h.* 'You are a very jabbering man.' *Tū kai dugā iā ushpē pā vich: tū pâ vilom.* 'Why do you kick my horse? I will kick you.' *Tū iā kai dugā oren vich? Tū iā oren vichibâ ō tū jārlam.* 'Why are you pushing me? If you push me I will do for you.'

A race difficult to ingratiate oneself with by small talk: *Tō'st kaz̲hīr krui p'ptī tā chuk z̲hi prots as̲ht?* 'How many black spots are there on your white dog's back?' was the friendly inquiry to which came the chilling reply: *Iā krūi brobar adr rang azzā: s̲htring na ass.* 'He is a yellow dog all over, and not spotted.'

from *The Frontier Scouts* by Charles Chenevix-Trench
(1919–21)

Lord Curzon, something of an expert on the Pamirs and the Hindu Kush (unique among Viceroys and policy-makers, he had actually ridden and walked over them), took very seriously the danger of invasion from Russian Turkestan, through the narrow panhandle of the Afghan Wakhan and over the Hindu Kush. The history of Russian expansion emphasised the danger. It is the task of general staffs to plan for the worst possible eventuality, which here would be Russian and Afghan invasion, assisted by the

Pathans of Dir and Swat through which must pass any force moving up from India to Chitral. There were at least three routes – by the Killick pass into Gilgit and the Baroghil and Dorah passes into Chitral – which could be easily defended, but if left undefended were perfectly practicable for trained mountain troops with mule transport.

It was against such a contingency that the local Political Agent suggested in 1900 the formation of a part-time militia of 'trained cragsmen' from the tough mountaineers of Chitral. It was a proposal after Lord Curzon's heart, a loyal militia defending their own country until regular troops could arrive, and it was the genesis of the Chitral Scouts, tribesmen armed with modern rifles, trained for one month a year and providing at a very small cost a tripwire which could at least delay an incursion. In 1913 the Gilgit Scouts were raised on similar lines with a similar role.

[The tribal police in Waziristan were known as Khassadars, and were generally considered unreliable. However there were exceptions, and one of them was . . .]

Ahwaz Khan, a hefty man with a permanent stubble on his chin. Of a Mahsud family who were hamsayas of the Tori Khel Wazirs, he got on well with both tribes. He spoke some English, and was popular with British troops who knew him as 'George'. One day he was escorting a three-car convoy from Bannu to Razmak when the second car was fired on, one officer, a sergeant and the driver being killed, and another officer wounded. 'George' at once stopped the leading car, which could have been driven to safety, and engaged the gang, defending the wounded officer until help arrived. On another occasion, when the Sappers had failed to defuse a 250-lb aircraft bomb placed to blow up a culvert, George tied his pagri round it and pulled it away. He was awarded the Albert Medal, later exchanged for the appropriately named George Medal. After being invested with it at Government House, he put on a sort of Jeeves act and bustled round handing out cigarettes and drinks. With all the appearance of a cheerful rogue, he was a brave and honest man.

from *On Honourable Terms*
The Memoirs of some Indian Police Officers, 1915–1948
edited by Martin Wynne

In 1935, when Benton was SP Jubbulpore, he was informed by the City Superintendent, Ali Akhtar, that there was evidence to suppose that a widow would become suttee at her husband's funeral that day. The burning ghats were situated on the banks of the Narbadda River, which is high on the list of holy rivers, and runs some five miles south of Jubbulpore on the Nagpur road. This road led from Jubbulpore to a collection of buildings and some beautiful temples with stone terraces and steps to the water. A few shops still existed where suttee ceremonies had taken place in the past. Ali Akhtar had already given orders to the Police Lines to despatch two squads of the Special Armed Force, under a sergeant and the Cantonment Inspector, by bus to the spot. He and Benton drove there immediately by car.

About a mile short of the river they met the police bus returning. In it was the Cantonment Inspector, the widow, her party of relatives and Brahmins, and a couple of constables. Inspector Osbourne said that on his arrival the suttee party and a crowd of Hindus had been inclined to resent interference, but as the police had been prepared to take firm action the funeral party had climbed into the bus without further delay. He thought that the widow, although closely veiled, was almost certainly drugged but was possibly quite a willing participant. The pyre had been practically ready for the torch.

It was in the woman's own interests that for the time being her whereabouts should be known to as few people as possible, and

[121]

the family and the Brahmins were only too willing to co-operate. Inspector Osbourne took away his bus load to an arranged destination while Benton and Ali Akhtar went onto the burning ghat. The sergeant was there with the police party and reported that the crowd had begun to disperse soon after the bus had left. He was told to remain there until the place was empty. Benton pays particular tribute to Ali Akhtar and Osbourne for their prompt, tactful and efficient handling of the situation, which prevented a serious crime and a possible religious riot.

from my diary . . .

When the missionary Edwina Crane commits suttee, by burning herself to death in her garden-shed (*Jewel in the Crown*), her devoted Christian servant Joseph, kneels helplessly by her pyre, muttering 'Oh madam . . . madam'.

Joseph was played by one of the waiters from the hotel where the cast stayed. We nicknamed him B.J., short for B. J. Bannerjee. He was coincidentally a Christian, and superficially more suited to playing Joseph than to his job as a waiter, in which role he suggested very strongly that he was not the horse to back.

He had a drooping black moustache, which increased the lugubriousness of his already lugubrious face. He shuffled along like a silent film comic, looking depressed and older than his fellow waiters, dowdy and moth-eaten. His oiled, stringy black hair was swept straight back, hanging too long and lank over neglected soft-white collars, too large for his ageing neck, around which they were gathered by a thin black tie. He did not have false teeth, but sounded as though he wore dentures.

I do not recall dandruff on his thinning lapels, but it would not have been out of place. He was 48, and looked ten years older, although his melancholic eyes concealed a rather surprising sense of humour.

With our 'back-from-shooting' sundowners, after a day's work, we always ordered nuts – warm, salted cashews. B.J. made a game of forgetting them.

'You haven't brought the nuts B.J.'.

'Oh shir, how shorry. Did you order nutsh?'

As Joseph, B.J. was required to witness what turned out to be an alarming conflagration. The flames began inside the shed – just as if Miss Crane herself was in there. Gradually tongues of fire began to flick between the gaps in the panels, and then, suddenly, the whole shed exploded into a swirling pillar of flame and black smoke.

Jon Woods, the camera-operator, who was fifteen yards downwind, was forced to move the camera back from the intense heat. B.J., upwind, mumbled on, his hands raised in prayer, the make-up department's tears flowing down his face. When there was nothing but the smouldering skeleton of the shed left, Ronald Merrick entered the shot, simply to inspect. On the coach home, I sat with B.J. and asked him if he was alright. He replied, beaming: 'Oh yesh, shir! I am very happy for my shot with you'.

It transpired that he later spent 17 rupees 95 paese (just over a pound), an amount about which he was meticulous, on medication for his face, which began to hurt him during the night. It was not serious and the company reimbursed him. I mention it because the other members of the hotel staff, most of whom found their way into the film, accused B.J. of using the incident to attract attention and ingratiate himself. I suspect their real motive was jealousy. Dog-eared, old B.J. was our overall favourite.

One day he said to me: 'Pleash, shir. You come to my humble home. It ish only poor man'sh food, but you come pleash. I am poor man, but I have a good heart'.

He also invited Ruth from make-up, Geraldine James, and

[123]

Charles Dance, whom he called Mishter Charlesh, and worshipped. We had an unforgettable evening with his family, and felt as attached to him, I think, as Miss Crane felt to her devoted Joseph.

When I was in Simla, later in the filming, I received this letter, on hotel notepaper, written in an easy, if irregular longhand, on pencilled guidelines.

Dear Brother, Tim Pigott-Smith
   I will not get your letter. I don't have words to express my feeling for you may god shower a lot of happiness on you, and you keep on progressing I wished I had enough money to come to simla to see you. I wish you could come once again to Udaipur after your shooting program Evary one in my family remamber you Please send me your adress in your next shooting. I can write your next letter.
   Please do reply. I am waiting for your reply Rest is ok with regards.

Yours
B. Bannerjee

BOMBAY from *Splendours of the Raj* by Philip Davies (1985)

Bombay resembles Victorian London not just in its civic architecture, but in its exuberance, colour and sheer dynamism. Both grew up with the same *laissez-faire* ethos, and both underwent similar attempts at civic improvement by well-meaning philanthropists and officials, but the difference is that in London the process continued. Gradually order was imposed on chaos and the congeries of uses and activities were unwound one by one. In Bombay this never happened, and it retains all the characteristics of the Victorian city, good and bad. As the wealth of the city increased, social problems of overcrowding, poor sanitation and epidemic disease rose in direct proportion. In 1864–65 there was a serious cholera outbreak, but the average annual death rate remained below that of London for many years, until improving environmental standards at home tipped the balance of figures against Bombay. As the programme of civic improvement gathered momentum Western innovations, such as gas lighting, were introduced. A portion of the town was lit in October 1866 and, as the lamplighters went from lamp to lamp, 'they were followed by crowds of inquisitive natives who gazed in mute astonishment at the new western wonder that had appeared in their midst.'

Colonel His Highness Shri Sir Ranjitsinhji Vibhaji, Maharajah Jam Saheb of Nawanagar, GBE, KCSI, was described by G. L. Jessop as 'the most brilliant figure in what I believe to be cricket's most brilliant period'. He was undoubtedly a great and innovative cricketer, and was known, to the British public, quite simply, as Ranji.

from *Ranji* by Alan Ross (1983)

But the circumstances of an Indian playing for England were ones never before considered. In 1896, and it was the last year in which this was the case, Test teams were not chosen by an independent selection committee, but by the county at whose ground the match was to be played. Thus MCC, whose President was the Lord Harris, six years previously Governor of Bombay, were responsible for the team for Lord's, Lancashire for the Old Trafford side, Surrey for the final Test at the Oval.

    Lord Harris was not, in fact, in favour of playing what he called 'birds of passage', and Ranji, though asked to make himself

[125]

available, was not chosen for the Lord's Test, an omission that resulted in public and press outcry. Some thirty years later Duleepsinhji, Ranji's much cherished nephew and little less a player, played in the first Test against South Africa but, objected to by the South Africans, agreed to stand down for the rest of the series.

The Australians, when Ranji was selected to play in the second Test at Old Trafford three weeks later, raised no such objections. Ranji, on being invited, insisted that the Australians should be consulted. They were, Trott expressed his delight, and no more was heard of the matter.

A. G. Gardner, the essayist, describes his batting style in the *Daily News*.

There is extraordinarily little display in his methods. He combines an Oriental calm with an Oriental swiftness – the stillness of the panther with the suddenness of its spring. He has none of the fine flourishes of our own stylists, but a quite startling economy of action . . . He stands moveless as the bowler approaches the wicket. He remains moveless as the ball is delivered. It seems to be upon him before he takes action. Then, without any preliminary flourish, the bat flashes to the ball, and the stroke is over. The body seems never to have changed its position, the feet are unmoved, the bat is as before . . . If the supreme art is to achieve the maximum result with the minimum expenditure of effort, the Jam Saheb, as a batsman, is in a class by himself . . . It is the art of the great etcher who with a line reveals infinity . . . The typical batsman performs a series of intricate evolutions in playing the ball; the Jam Saheb flicks his wrist and the ball bounds to the ropes. It is not jugglery, or magic; it is simply the perfect economy of a means to an end.

from *Plain Tales from the Raj* by C. H. Allen (1977)

H. E. Wickham describes the Maharajah of Kashmir . . .

At three o'clock in the afternoon that Maharajah himself would come down to the ground, the band would play the Kashmir anthem, salaams were made and he then went off to a special tent where he sat for a time, smoking his long water-pipe. At four thirty or thereabouts he decided he would bat. It didn't matter which side was batting, his own team or ours. He was padded by two attendants and gloved by two more, somebody carried his bat and he walked out to the wicket looking very dignified, very small and with an enormous turban on his head. In one of the matches I happened to be bowling and my first ball hit his stumps, but the wicket keeper, quick as lightning, shouted 'No Ball!' and the match went on. The only way that the Maharajah could get out was by lbw. And after fifteen or twenty minutes batting he said he felt tired and he was duly given out lbw. What the scorers did about his innings, which was never less than half a century, goodness only knows.

Love

from the *Kama Sutra*
translated by Sir Richard Burton and F. F. Arbuthnot (1883)

On the different Kinds of Love

Men learned in the humanities are of opinion that love is of four kinds:

Love acquired by continual habit
Love resulting from the imagination
Love resulting from belief
Love resulting from the perception of external objects

Love resulting from the constant and continual performance of some act is called love acquired by constant practice and habit, as for instance the love of sexual intercourse, the love of hunting, the love of drinking, the love of gambling, etc., etc.

Love which is felt for things to which we are not habituated, and which proceeds entirely from ideas, is called love resulting from imagination, as for instance that love which some men and women and eunuchs feel for the Auparishtaka or mouth congress, and that which is felt by all for such things as embracing, kissing, etc., etc.

The love which is mutual on both sides, and proved to be true, when each looks upon the other as his or her very own, such is called love resulting from belief by the learned.

The love resulting from the perception of external objects is quite evident and well known to the world, because the pleasure which it affords is superior to the pleasure of the other kinds of love, which exists only for its sake.

What has been said in this chapter upon the subject of sexual union is sufficient for the learned; but for the edification of the ignorant, the same will now be treated of at length and in detail.

[131]

Marriage, from *Hindu Holiday* by J. R. Ackerley (1932)

1. Betrothal

A Hindoo marriage, he said, is divided into three ceremonies – Betrothal, Marriage, and Consummation; and the first of these takes place when the boy is about five years old. At about that time his father begins to look about for a wife for him, and this is sometimes done by means of a messenger – a professional matchmaker – who visits the district in search of a baby girl of suitable rank – that is to say, of at least equal caste.

This is the most important consideration. Usually, I suppose, the two families are neighbours, well known to each other, and already perhaps in agreement on this question, so that the employment of a messenger is either unnecessary or a mere formality; but when there is no such familiarity, some inquiry is necessary.

Either this inquiry is considered sufficiently answered by information brought by the messenger, or sometimes an actual inspection of the would-be bride is thought desirable; at any rate Romance can obviously have no part in the transaction, and when the boy's family have ascertained that, besides being of the right caste, the girl is a strong and serviceable article, sound in mind and limb, and in possession of her faculties, then they have learned about her all that they have any wish to know. But, as Babaji Rao observed, it is now different in his more advanced society; a photograph is usually required, and, if this is not forthcoming, some *serious* member of the family – the father, or the elder brother (the younger brother is not considered serious) – will visit the young lady and report upon her appearance. After this, if the reports from both sides are satisfactory, her father will wish to examine the horoscope of the prospective bridegroom to see whether it is favourable and agrees with that of his daughter; and if there is anything wrong, if the boy's horoscope predicts for him an early grave, or if, however unexceptionable it may be in

[132]

itself, in conjunction with the girl's equally good horoscope it prognosticates a barren or unhappy union, the marriage is off. All Hindoo children have a horoscope taken at birth, except the lowest castes, sweepers and cobblers, who usually cannot afford the services of a pundit, and are therefore obliged to go through life without knowing, from day to day, what is about to happen to them.

But if the two horoscopes are harmonious the marriage is arranged, the actual proposal always coming from the girl's side, and the betrothal ceremony takes place. Later on they are married.

from the Vaishnava poetry of Bengal (*c.* 1500 AD)
translated by Edward Dimock and Denise Levertov

This is a very tailored selection of these poems. The aim of my editing is simply to make available the passages more easily comprehensible without a deeper understanding of Hindu culture. My own knowledge is shallow, and if I give offence to others by my editing, I apologise. Madhava is another name for the God of Love, Krishna. The speaker is Radha, who is, naturally, in love with him, and describes her joining him under the cover of night.

O Madhava, how shall I tell you of my terror?
I could not describe my coming here
if I had a million tongues.
When I left my room and saw the darkness I trembled:
I could not see the path, there were snakes that
    writhed around my ankles!

[133]

I was alone, a woman! the night was so dark,
the forest so dense and gloomy,
and I had far to go.
The rain was pouring down –
which path should I take?
My feet were muddy
and burning where thorns had scratched them.
   But I had the hope of seeing you, none of it mattered,
and now my terror seems far away . . .
When the sound of your flute reaches my ears
it compels me to leave my home, my friends,
it draws me into the dark toward you.

O Madhava, never let our love
seem to grow stale –
I beg you, let the dew
not dry on our flowers,
that my honour be not destroyed.

Only my life is left – and my life too
is only a breath that is leaving me.

When he heard these words from her beautiful mouth, Madhava
      bowed his head. He knew he held the flower of her life
                        in his keeping.

(Krishna replies)

             My moon-faced one,
             I am waiting
                   to make our bed ready
                   to gather lotus petals –
             your body will press them,
             hidden from even friendly eyes . . .
             Come,

the sweet breeze from the sandalwoods
censes our trysting place . . .

from *Hindu Holiday*

2. Marriage

On the day fixed for this second ceremony the bridegroom goes
with his parents and a great company to the house of the bride's
father. But he does not enter it in company. At some distance
from it the party halts, and he goes on alone and empty-handed,
for it is the custom that he should seem to arrive a beggar and that
the girl should be given to him for charity's sake. In the bride's
house a great company meet the bridegroom, and another house
is allotted to him and his friends, since he will have to stay and
feast for some days. This is usually in the spring, the most
propitious time for marriages.

The actual ceremony is rather complicated, but as far as I
remember, the couple sit on the floor and a sacred fire is lighted
between them by the officiating pundit. They then rise and unite –
that is to say, their vestments are tied together by a piece of
consecrated cloth beneath which their hands are joined – and
walk three times round the sacred fire, each time in seven steps,
repeating prayers and Vedic hymns. This concludes the ceremony; they are now man and wife, and he takes her with him
back to his home, where she stays for a couple of days in order to
meet his relations.

Marriage by Nissim Ezekiel (1960)

Lovers, when they marry, face
Eternity with touching grace.
Complacent at being fated
Never to be separated.

The bride is always pretty, the groom
A lucky man. The darkened room
Roars out the joy of flesh and blood.
The use of nakedness is good.

I went through this, believing all,
Our love denied the Primal Fall.
Wordless, we walked among the trees,
And felt immortal as the breeze.

However many times we came
Apart, we came together. The same
Thing over and over again.
Then suddenly the mark of Cain

Began to show on her and me.
Why should I ruin the mystery
By harping on the suffering rest,
Myself a frequent wedding guest?

from *Hindu Holiday*

3. Consummation

The marriage is not, of course, consummated; this is another
business altogether, and happens one year, three years, or five

[136]

years later, at the discretion of the parents. If it is a lower-class marriage the wife has complete freedom and may go where she likes (though she will probably veil her face before any strange and undue interest in the streets); but if she is of the upper classes she disappears, after the consummation ceremony, into *purdah*, and save by her husband, her near relations, and female friends, is never seen again.

'And, provided there is no fundamental incompatibility, nor any physical repulsion on either side, love,' said Babaji Rao complacently, 'comes of its own accord.'

by Nissim Ezekiel

This, she said to herself,
As she sat at table
With the English boss,
Is IT. This is the promise:
The long evenings
In the large apartment
With cold beer and Western music,
Lucid talk of art and literature,
And of all 'the changes India needs'.

At the second meeting
In the large apartment
After cold beer and the music on,
She sat in disarray.
The struggle had been hard
And not altogether successful.
Certainly the blouse
Would not be used again.

But with true British courtesy
He lent her a safety pin
Before she took the elevator down.

from *The Bhagavad Gita* (*c.* 500 BC)

Water flows continually into the ocean
But the ocean is never disturbed:
Desire flows into the mind of the seer
But he is never disturbed.
The seer knows peace:
The man who stirs up his own lusts
Can never know peace.
He knows peace who has forgotten desire.
He lives without craving:
Free from ego, free from pride.

A Letter to a Friend by Arvind Krishna Mehrotra (1976)

I set up the house while she waited
In another city, the day of our marriage
Was still far. When she saw the rooms
For the first time she said, 'These
Are worse than bathrooms.'
She found the walls too narrow and wanted
To run away; your mother and my aunt
Were both there when this happened.
Your mother in her enthusiasm
And simple joy

[138]

Asked us over for lunch
When she said, 'I know nothing of lunches.'
It was months before things got normal again.
Anyhow, she spent her first days
With the clear sky, a few birds, the little
Interesting things which gather
Around trees; we slept in the afternoon
And awoke when the long, sad evening
Was already halfway up the window.
Kitchen smoke, the quiet smell
Of me reading in my chair, the glum
Books that smacked their tails
On the shelves like field-mice, the family
Downstairs quarrelling and crying,
Poisoned the tips of needles in her mind
And she entered an imprisoned kingdom –
A place I wouldn't touch with my bare hands.
Through two short rooms she walked
As if I were out to murder her last secret
And a blackness we all feel took hold of me;
I wanted it to, to protect myself;
Her eyes glistened, scared, scary.
At night insects on wings and feet would come
To relieve the stiff air; we played
Under the sharp moon, made little noise
Since I hardly touched her.
The first caw and the excitement
Of crows as they looked at us in bed from the chimney,
Bees rushed into the room, the sun pulled up,
And the girl next door wrung her underwear;
She knew I admired her ankles even in sleep.
The milkwoman brought her dog with her,
The postman came up the steps and she spent
Hours reading letters from her family,
Then wrote to each one of her brothers and sisters.

[139]

The lama would knock and take off his shoes
Before entering; he would hold her hand and talk
Of silence, of living in the mountains
With just enough candles to scatter the dark.
We fetched water in heavy buckets, cooked
In the open, and lying on the hillside
None thought of love.
She made tea by boiling
Water, leaves, milk and sugar
Together, adding condiments in the end;
When he left, her palms were wet
And I wasn't jealous.
Across the clean flat roofs and narrow road
Is a bare field; a camel once sat there all day,
Thin legs folded under the hump,
Looking at cows walk through trees.
So has it been.
Her blood has got more entangled in its stones,
While I've kept to my lamp, beads, mirrors, jars,
A rug, pictures of purple demons,
Red, black, and white ants, all sorts of fat spiders.
Three years, and I still wonder
What nakedness is, or does.
Sometimes I notice the couple next door.
It's very warm outside,
And the streets are tall and quiet.

by Nissim Ezekiel

I like this little poem, she said,
when did you write it?
My only haiku, that went:
Unasked, as the day
declined, she brought out her small
breasts, to be caressed.
I'm glad you like it,
smiling weakly, intrigued.
What exactly is a haiku?
And when I told her,
she repeated, I like it.
Unasked, as the day
declined, she brought out her full
breasts, to be caressed.

Love among the Pines by Keki Daruwalla (1982)

The animal evening moves
like the tiger-wind through the parting of reeds.
The sky is not blue enough today
to catch the pure spiral of your thought.
We walk in the cowdust, my fingers
lost in the spaces between your fingers.
Some wild flowers catch your eye
and I sleepwalk through
some moments of wild talk about
    wild flowers from you.
What makes me whisper
    destiny lies
  in the parting of hair
  in the parting of grasses

in the parting of thighs?
Dusk explodes into black shrapnel
on the knife-rim of the earth.
What is there in my hand that when it sidles into your blouse
it prowls like an animal that makes you writhe,
turning your nipples into a black sprout of berries?
We sweep pineneedles into a stack
(they don't prick at all when vertically spread).
The pinecricket overhead is a shrill monotone.
The moments stacked against each other
turn incandescent with a running flame.
We both know what we are here for:
     beneath your skin
of wild talk you are tense,
beneath the cindering ash of my body
your body is a surprise
for as I fall upon the earth-crust that is you
we spin, we spin, we spin
your feet pointed to the skies.

More of the Vaishnava poetry. Radha again speaks to Krishna . . .

Lord of my heart, what have I dreamed . . .
how shall I go home, now that daylight has come?
My musk and sandalwood perfumes are faded,
the kohl smudged from my eyes, the vermilion line
drawn in the part of my hair, paled.
O put the ornament
of your own body upon me,
take me with you down-glancing one.

[142]

Dress me in your own yellow robes,
smooth my dishevelled hair,
wind round my throat your garland of forest flowers.

Her cloud of hair eclipses the lustre of her face, like Rahu
    greedy for the moon;
the garland glitters in her unbound hair, a wave of the Ganges in
    the waters of the Yamuna.
How beautiful the deliberate sensuous union of the two; the girl
    playing this time the active role,
riding her lover's outstretched body in delight;
her smiling lips shine with drops of sweat; the god of love
    offering pearls to the moon.
She of beautiful face hotly kisses the mouth of her beloved; the
    moon with face bent down, drinks of the lotus.
The garland hanging on her heavy breasts seems like a stream of
    milk from golden jars.
The tinkling bells which decorate her hips sound the triumphal
    music of the god of love

> When they had made love
> she lay in his arms in the kunja grove.
> Suddenly she called his name
> and wept – as if she burned in the fire of
> separation.

(and when they are apart) . . .

> O my friend, my sorrow is unending.
> It is the rainy season, my house is empty,
> the sky is filled with seething clouds,
> the earth sodden with rain,
> and my love far away.

[143]

Cruel Kama pierces me with his arrows:
the lightning flashes, the peacocks dance,
frogs and waterbirds, drunk with delight,
call incessantly – and my heart is heavy.
Darkness on earth,
the sky intermittently lit with a sullen glare.

from The Meghaduta of Kalidasa . . .

The Transport of Love by Kalidasa (c. 400 AD)
translated from the Sanskrit by Leonard Nathan

The Meghaduta's entire 'action' is embodied in the long
apostrophe of an exiled minor deity, or Yaksha, who
asks that a cloud carry his message of devotion
to his far-off mate.

1

This Yaksha, banished a desolate year
from his love and from the king whose curse
for some carelessness sent him impotent away,
spent his exile among the holy retreats
of Rāmagiri where Sītā, bathing, had made
the waters holy and where trees cast a rich shade.

2

On this mountain, months from his mate,
aching for love, his wrist so wasted
that the gold bracelet he wore slipped off

[144]

and was lost – he saw at summer's end
a cloud swelling against the peak
like a great elephant nuzzling a hill.

3

So he stood there, shaken, this courtier
of Kubera, his tears held back, considering
that heart-breaking sight a long time.
A sudden cloud can mute the mind
of the happiest man – how much more
when the one he is dying to hold is far from him.

4

Knowing the rains were near, desperate to keep
his love alive and thinking this cloud
could carry her news of how he was –
he offered it fresh blossoms
of the kuṭ'aja and, gladdened now,
welcomed it with warm words.

5

What does a cloud – a mix of vapor,
flame, water, and wind – have to do with messages
made to be sent by beings fit to bear them?
But still the Yaksha implored it. Those
sick with desire can no longer tell
what will answer and what is dumb.

6

'I know you born of a famous race of clouds
called "The Whirlpools" and high minister to Indra,
able to take any shape you will – so I
who am far from love by a fatal order,
implore you. Better a futile prayer
to greatness than the full favor of boors.'

[145]

7

O, Cloud, remedy for those fevered with pain,
carry a message for me who am cut off
from my love by the fury of Kubera. You must go
To a city called Alaka where the mansions of Yaksha lords
are rinsed by moonlight beamed from the brow
of Shiva, whose home is an outlying grove.

Bhagavad Gita (c. 500 BC)

The wind turns a ship
From its course upon the waters:
The wandering winds of the senses
Cast man's mind adrift
And turn his better judgment from its course.
When a man can still the senses
I call him illumined.
The recollected mind is awake
In the knowledge of the Atman*
Which is dark night to the ignorant:
The ignorant are awake in their sense-life
Which they think is daylight:
To the seer it is darkness.

* The Atman is the godhead within every being.

Bonds of Hatred

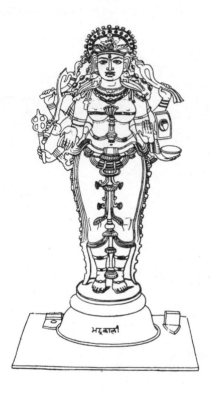

भद्रकाली

A war and traffic are incompatible. By my consent, ye shall no way engage yourselves but at sea, where you are like to gain as often as to lose. It is the beggaring of the Portugal . . . It hath been also the error of the Dutch, who seek plantation here by the sword . . . Let this be received as a rule, that, if you will profit, seek it at sea, and in quiet trade; for without controversy it is an error to affect garrisons and land wars in India.

Sir Thomas Roe

who helped establish the English merchant-trade
in India during the years 1615–1619

from the diary . . .

Our location moved to Seringapatnam, near Mysore. It was in itself a famous grave, where the Moslem ruler and Indian national hero Tipu Sultan – the Tiger of Mysore – had finally been defeated by the British in 1799.

Tipu had been on the rampage against the British invaders ever since his defeat by Cornwallis in 1793, aided by the French with whom he allied. The English lined up with the Nizam of Hyderabad. It was an appalling situation in which the English and the French, who were anyway ruthlessly sharing out the remnants of the collapsing Mogul Empire, found themselves at war in India largely because they were at war with each other in Europe. The commander of the England/Hyderabad force died as a result of injuries sustained in a duel, and one of the men who consequently enjoyed promotion was the young Arthur Wellesley, later the Duke of Wellington. He had arrived in India on a slow troop ship which left the Cape in September 1796, and reached India in February 1797 – five months later!

On his way south from Hyderabad to Mysore, with the army, and a 120,000 strong train of bullocks, few of which survived the journey, Wellesley managed to avoid being pinned in the jungle by Tipu's elephants, but learnt a dreadful lesson from Tipu at Sultanpettah Tope.

Wellesley had been ordered to lead his men through the unfamiliar ground of the Tope: there had been no reconnoitre, and it was night time. Tipu played havoc with them, and many died. Wellesley was very shaken by the experience, and the military stupidity. He vowed never again to approach a well-situated enemy over unfamiliar ground by night – it seems obvious enough really – and of course, Wellesley never broke his word.

Tipu's fort at Seringapatnam was on an island in the River

Cauvery, but the English soon broke the siege, when one of their rockets blew up Tipu's magazine. The Tiger fought valiantly and bloodily to his death, and then the English moved in. The treasure was estimated at £1,143,216 – not bad for 1799. Wellesley personally received £4,000. The sepoys got £5 each.

We were filming on the Wellesley Bridge – a magnificent old stone bridge, a hundred yards long, which spanned the wide and shallow River Cauvery, in which water buffalo lounged, washer-women washed, and naked boys played and swam.

In our film, this bridge is used as the Bibighar bridge – the bridge linking the white cantonment with the black town – and it is over this bridge that Hari Kumar runs.

from *the Raj Quartet* by Paul Scott (1966)

At his English public school, Chillingborough, Hari Kumar was known as Coomer. Guy Perron remembers him playing cricket . . .

For a while pictures of the day just ended flickered across the screen lowered by his eyelids, but all at once there was the disturbing invasion of shots of Coomer, from all angles, long, medium and close; Coomer opening his shoulders, hitting out at a sequence of balls whose pitch and pace were subtly varied by the invisible bowler; or team of bowlers; the deliveries were in too mercilessly rapid a succession for one man alone to send down.

The cameras of Perron's imagination began to tire. Presently only one remained, and this zoomed in close to recreate a memory of the boy's face. There was a face, an idea of a face, a man's rather than a boy's, and formed from a notion of an expression rather than from one of features: an expression of concentration, of hard-held determination, of awareness that to misjudge, to

[150]

mistime, would lead to destruction. There was no sound. And suddenly the face vanished. A flurry of birds, crows, rooks, rose from the surrounding elms, startled by a sudden noise, although there had been no noise. And they were not elms, but palms; and the birds were kite-hawks. They circled patiently above Perron's head, waiting for him to fall asleep.

Struggling with the unfamiliar heat of India, poor Hari is haunted by dreams of England.

His sharpest memories were of piles of leaves, wet and chill to the touch, as if in early morning after a late October frost. To Hari, England was sweet cold and crisp clean pungent scent; air that moved, crowding hollows and sweeping hilltops; not stagnant, heavy, a conducting medium for stench. And England was the park and pasture-land behind the house in Sidcot, the gables of the house, the leaded diamond-pane windows, and the benevolent wistaria.

   Waking in the middle of the night on the narrow string-bed in his room at Number 12 Chillianwallah Bagh he beat at the mosquitoes, fisted his ears against the sawing of the frogs and the chopping squawk of the lizards in heat on the walls and ceiling. He entered the mornings from tossing dreams of home and slipped at once into the waking nightmare, his repugnance for everything the alien country offered: the screeching crows outside and the fat amber-coloured cockroaches that lumbered heavy-backed but light-headed with waving feathery antennae from the bedroom to an adjoining bathroom where there was no bath – instead, a tap, a bucket, a copper scoop, a cemented floor to stand on and a slimy runnel for taking the dirty water out through a hole in the wall from which it fell and spattered the caked mud of the compound; draining him layer by layer of his Englishness.

Pagett M. P. by Rudyard Kipling (1885–1912)

Pagett, M. P., was a liar, and a fluent liar therewith, –
He spoke of the heat of India as 'The Asian Solar Myth';
Came on a four months' visit, to 'study the East' in November,
And I got him to make an agreement vowing to stay till
    September.

March came in with the *koïl*.* Pagett was cool and gay,
Called me a 'bloated Brahmin,' talked of my 'princely pay.'
March went out with the roses. 'Where is your heat?' said he.
'Coming,' said I to Pagett. 'Skittles!' said Pagett, M. P.

April began with the punkah, coolies, and prickly-heat, –
Pagett was dear to mosquitoes, sandflies found him a treat.
He grew speckled and lumpy – hammered, I grieve to say,
Aryan brothers who fanned him, in an illiberal way.

May set in with a dust-storm, – Pagett went down with the sun.
All the delights of the season tickled him one by one.
Imprimis – ten days' 'liver' – due to his drinking beer;
Later, a dose of fever – slight, but he called it severe.

Dysent'ry touched him in June, after the *Chota Bursat**
Lowered his portly person – made him yearn to depart.
He didn't call me a 'Brahmin,' or 'bloated,' or 'overpaid,'
But seemed to think it a wonder that any one ever stayed.

July was a trifle unhealthy, – Pagett was ill with fear,
Called it the 'Cholera Morbus,' hinted that life was dear.
He babbled of 'Eastern exile,' and mentioned his home with
    tears;
But I hadn't seen *my* children for close upon seven years.

*The early rains.

[152]

We reached a hundred and twenty once in the Court at noon,
[I've mentioned Pagett was portly] Pagett went off in a swoon.
That was an end to the business. Pagett, the perjured, fled
With a practical, working knowledge of 'Solar Myths' in his
  head.

And I laughed as I drove from the station, but the mirth died out
  on my lips
As I thought of the fools like Pagett who write of their 'Eastern
  trips,'
And the sneers of the travelled idiots who duly misgovern the
  land,
And I prayed to the Lord to deliver another one into my hand.

from *They called me an 'IMPECCABLE IMPERIALIST'*
by Lionel Jardine Indian Civil Service (Ret'd) (1979)

We were not totally unprepared, though our servants were
amazed, when Dr Ghosh arrived one afternoon at our home,
dressed wholly in hand-woven cloth and with a Congress flag on
the radiator of his tiny 'Baby' Austin car.

He opened the conversation by saying that he was surprised
that a British officer should claim to be living by standards of love
and unselfishness, when just such a British officer and his
colleagues were instigating Muslim tribesmen to murder and rob
his Hindu co-religionists. This sudden and direct attack took
me aback and I felt my temper rising. But I remembered Dr
Buchman once warning me, 'You may win the argument, but you
lose the man.' So I controlled my temper and confined myself to
saying I could understand there must be lots of things about the
British that were likely to offend Indians. I invited him to come

[153]

again when I had more leisure and have a talk. Rather to my surprise he accepted my invitation.

Thereafter he began to visit our home and sometimes read to my wife a speech he intended to make in the Assembly. His speeches in the past had been definitely divisive. He wanted my wife to help him to introduce a more positive note. He began to trust us and other British people he met with us. One day I asked him whether he still believed we instigated the tribesmen to kill Hindus. 'Of course I don't,' he said. 'But my friends still do.'

Written by F. Engels on May 8, 1858
Published in the New York Daily Tribune, No. 5333
of May 25, 1858, as a leading article.

If the reckless soldiery, in their civilizing and humanizing progress through India, could rob the natives of their personal property only, the British Government steps in immediately afterward and strips them of their real estate as well. Talk of the First French Revolution confiscating the lands of the nobles and the church! Talk of Louis Napoleon confiscating the property of the Orleans family! Here comes Lord Canning, a British nobleman, mild in language, manners and feelings, and confiscates, by order of his superior, Viscount Palmerston, the lands of a whole people, every rood, perch and acre, over an extent of ten thousand square miles. A very nice bit of *loot* indeed for John Bull! And no sooner has Lord Ellenborough, in the name of the new Government, disapproved of this hitherto unexampled measure, than up rise *The Times* and a host of minor British papers to defend this wholesale robbery, and break a lance for the right of John Bull to confiscate everything he likes. But then, John is an exceptional being, and what is virtue in him, according to *The Times*, would be infamy in others.

A complaint by Bengali ruler, about the activities of
Robert Clive, and other British nabobs.

They make a disturbance all over my country, plunder the people;
injure and disgrace my servants . . . Setting up the colours and
showing the passes of the Company they use their utmost en-
deavours to oppress the peasants, merchants and other people of
the country . . . They forcibly take away the goods of the peasants,
merchants etc for a fourth part of their value, and by ways of
violence and oppressions they oblige the peasants to give five
rupees for goods which are worth but one rupee and for the sale of
five rupees they bind and disgrace a man who pays a hundred
rupees in land-tax . . .

from *Portrait of India* by Ved Mehta (1970)

In 1756 the Nawab of Bengal attacked and captured the British
garrison of Fort William, Calcutta. This is an edited version
of a letter written by one of the few survivors, Mr J. Holwell,
magistrate:

The Nawab and his troops were in possession of the fort before
six in the evening. He repeated his assurances to me that no harm
should come to us; and indeed, I believe that his orders were only
general: that we should for the night be secured; and that what
followed was the result of 'revenge' and resentment in the breasts
of the lower Indian officers . . .

We were no sooner all within the barracks, than the guard

[155]

advanced to the inner arches and parapet wall: and with their muskets presented, ordered us to go into the room at the southernmost end of the barracks, commonly called the Black Hole prison.

I got possession of the window nearest the door, and took Messrs Coles and Scott with me, they being wounded.

Figure to yourself, if possible, the situation of a hundred and forty-six wretches, exhausted by continual fatigue and action, crammed together in a cube of about eighteen feet, on a close sultry night in Bengal. The moment I quitted the window, my breathing grew short and painful . . . I laid myself down on some of the dead behind me, and recommending myself to heaven, had the comfort of thinking my sufferings could have no long duration . . .

The Nawab, who had received an account of the havoc death had made among us, sent an order for our release near six in the morning . . .

The little strength remaining amongst the robust who survived, made it a difficult task to remove the dead piled up against the door; so that I believe it was more than twenty minutes before we obtained a passage out one at a time . . .

from *Recollections of my Life* by Joseph Frayer, Surgeon

Siege of Lucknow Residency, 1857.

The 2nd of July was the most eventful day during the siege, for a sad calamity overtook us. Sir Henry Lawrence, who was exhausted with work and heat lay down on a couch in the room through which the round-shot had passed the day before. An 8-inch shell came in through the window and exploded, filling the room with smoke, flame and debris. Captain Wilson, with one knee on the couch, was reading a memo to Sir Henry. He was knocked down, and then Sir Henry's voice was heard saying that he had been wounded. A native assistant who was in the room had his foot carried off by a fragment of the shell. Wilson was bruised, but George Lawrence was unhurt. They summoned assistance, carried Sir Henry into the drawing-room and laid him on a table, supporting him with pillows.

I found him lying as described. I saw he was seriously injured, for he was pale, his voice was low, he was semi-collapsed, and was talking in a hurried and excited manner. I did what was possible to arrest the haemorrhage, – there was not much, – to alleviate pain and relieve the condition of shock.

The principal officers were soon about him, and knowing he was dying, he directed Colonel Inglis to assume command of the troops. He was perfectly clear and collected, though much exhausted, and gave full instructions as to what he wished to be done. He most earnestly adjured us never to surrender or treat with the enemy, and to do everything possible to protect the women and children, to economise provisions and defend the Residency to the last or until relief should arrive. He took leave of us all in the most affecting manner, spoke most humbly of himself, and all that he had done, and expressed a desire that the only epitaph on his tomb should be,

'Here lies Henry Lawrence, who tried to do his duty.'

Defence of Lucknow by Lord Tennyson (1879)

I

Banner of England, not for a season, O banner of England, hast thou
Floated in conquering battle or flapt to the battle-cry!

Never with mightier glory than when we had rear'd thee on
   high,
Flying at top of the roofs in the ghastly siege of Lucknow –
   Shot thro' the staff or the halyard, but ever we raised thee
      anew,
   And ever upon the topmost roof our banner of England blew.

II

Frail were the works that defended the hold that we held with
   our lives –
Women and children among us, God help them, our children
   and wives!
Hold it we might – and for fifteen days or for twenty at most.
'Never surrender, I charge you, but every man die at his post!'
Voice of the dead whom we loved, our Lawrence the brave of
   the brave:
Cold were his brows when we kiss'd him – we laid him that night
   in his grave.
'Every man die at his post!' and there hail'd on our houses and
   halls
Death from their rifle-bullets, and death from their cannon balls,
Death in our innermost chamber, and death at our slight
   barricade,
Death while we stood with the musket, and death while we
   stoopt to the spade,
Death to the dying, and wounds to the wounded, for often there
   fell,
Striking the hospital wall, crashing thro' it, their shot and their
   shell,
Death, for their spies were among us, their marksmen were told
   of our best,
So that the brute bullet broke thro' the brain that could think for
   the rest;
Bullets would sing by our foreheads, and bullets would rain at
   our feet –

Fire from ten thousand at once of the rebels that girdled us
    round –
Death at the glimpse of a finger from over the breadth of a street,
    Death from the heights of the mosque and the palace, and
    death in the ground!
Mine? yes, a mine! Countermine! down, down! and creep thro'
    the hole!
Keep the revolver in hand! You can hear him – the murderous
    mole!
    Quiet, ah! quiet! wait till the point of the pickaxe be thro'!
Click with the pick, coming nearer and nearer again than
before –
Now let it speak, and you fire, and the dark pioneer is no more;
    And ever upon the topmost roof our banner of England blew!

III

Ay, but the foe sprung his mine many times, and it chanced on a
    day
Soon as the blast of that underground thunderclap echo'd away,
Dark thro' the smoke and the sulphur like so many fiends in
    their hell –
Cannon-shot, musket-shot, volley on volley, and yell upon yell –
Fiercely on all the defences our myriad enemy fell.
What have they done? where is it? Out yonder. Guard the
    Redan!
Storm at the Water-gate! storm at the Bailey-gate! storm, and it
    ran
Surging and swaying all round us, as ocean on every side
Plunges and heaves at a bank that is daily devour'd by the tide –
So many thousands that if they be bold enough, who shall
    escape?
    Kill or be kill'd, live or die, they shall know we are soldiers
    and men!
Ready! take aim at their leaders – their masses are gapp'd with
    our grape –

Backward they reel like the wave; like the wave flinging
    forward again,
Flying and foil'd at the last by the handful they could not
    subdue;
And ever upon the topmost roof our banner of England blew.

IV

Handful of men as we were, we were English in heart and in
    limb,
    Strong with the strength of the race to command, to obey, to
        endure,
Each of us fought as if hope for the garrison hung but on him;
    Still – could we watch at all points? we were every day fewer
        and fewer.
There was a whisper among us, but only a whisper that past:
    'Children and wives – if the tigers leap into the fold
unawares –
Every man die at his post – and the foe may outlive us at last.
    Better to fall by the hand that they love, than to fall into
        theirs!'
Roar upon roar, in a moment two mines by the enemy sprung
    Clove into perilous chasms our walls and our poor palisades.
Riflemen, true in your heart, but be sure that your hand be as
    true!
Sharp is the fire of assault, better aimed are your flank
fusillades –
    Twice do we hurl them to earth from the ladders to which
        they had clung,
Twice from the ditch where they shelter we drive them with
    hand-grenades;
    And ever upon the topmost roof our banner of England blew.

V

Then on another wild morning another wild earthquake
    out-tore

[160]

Clean from our lines of defence ten or twelve good paces or
    more.
Rifleman, high on the roof, hidden there from the light of the
    sun –
  One has leapt up on the breach, crying out: Follow me, follow
    me! –
  Mark him – he falls! then another, and *him* too, and down
    goes he.
Had they been bold enough then, who can tell but the traitors
    had won?
Boardings and rafters and doors – an embrasure! make way for
    the gun!
Now double-charge it with grape! it is charged and we fire, and
    they run.
Praise to our Indian brothers, and let the dark face have his due!
Thanks to the kindly dark faces who fought with us, faithful and
    few,
Fought with the bravest among us, and drove them, and smote
    them, and slew,
That ever upon the topmost roof our banner in India blew.

VI

Men will forget what we suffer and not what we do. We can
    fight!
But to be soldier all day and be sentinel all thro' the night –
Ever the mine and assault, our sallies, their lying alarms,
Bugles and drums in the darkness, and shoutings and soundings
    to arms,
Ever the labour of fifty that had to be done by five,
Ever the marvel among us that one should be left alive,
Ever the day with its traitorous death from the loopholes around,
Ever the night with its coffinless corpse to be laid in the ground,
Heat like the mouth of a hell, or a deluge of cataract skies,
Stench of old offal decaying, and infinite torment of flies,
Thoughts of the breezes of May blowing over an English field,

Cholera, scurvy, and fever, the wound that *would* never be
   heal'd;
Lopping away of the limb by the pitiful, pitiless knife, –
Torture and trouble in vain – for it never could save us a life.
Valour of delicate women who tended the hospital bed,
Horror of women in travail among the dying and dead,
Grief for our perishing children, and never a moment for grief,
Toil and ineffable weariness, faltering hopes of relief,
Havelock baffled, or beaten, or butcher'd for all that we knew –
   Then day and night, day and night, coming down on the
      still-shatter'd walls
   Millions of musket-bullets, and thousands of cannon-balls:
But ever upon the topmost roof our banner of England blew.

<h2 style="text-align:center">VII</h2>

Hark, cannonade, fusillade! is it true what was told by the scout,
   Outram and Havelock breaking their way through the fell
      mutineers?
   Surely the pibroch of Europe is ringing again in our ears!
All on a sudden the garrison utter a jubilant shout,
   Havelock's glorious Highlanders answer with conquering
      cheers,
Sick from the hospital answer them, women and children come
   out,
   Blessing the wholesome white faces of Havelock's good
      fusileers,
   Kissing the war-harden'd hand of the Highlander wet with
      their tears!
Dance to the pibroch! – saved! we are saved! – is it you? is it you?
   Saved by the valour of Havelock, saved by the blessing of
      heaven!
   'Hold it for fifteen days!' – we have held it for eighty-seven!
And ever aloft on the palace roof the old banner of England
   blew.

[162]

from *The Siege of Krishnaipur* by J. G. Farrell (1973)

The romantic aesthete, Fleury, finds himself in difficulty during the latter days of the siege.

Upstairs, Fleury had taken the pistol to pieces (as far as it could be taken to pieces which did not seem to be very far) and put it together again. He did not believe himself to be any the wiser as regards the reason for it not firing, but he thought he might as well try again.

'I say, you don't happen to know how this blessed thing works, do you?' he asked the person who had just come into the music-room. But he did not wait for a reply before throwing himself to one side as a sabre whistled down and buried itself deep in the brickwork of the window-sill where he had been sitting. Somehow a burly sepoy had found his way into the music-room; this man's only ambition appeared to be to cut Fleury in pieces. Luckily, the blade of the sabre had snapped off and remained embedded in the wall, giving Fleury time to aim the pistol and pull the trigger. But this time there was only a disappointing click; not even the percussion cap fired. Never mind, Fleury had plenty of other weapons. He was now trying to drag one of the wavy-bladed Malayan daggers out of his belt, which was actually a cummerbund; he was having difficulty, though, because the corrugated edges had got caught in his shirt. Well, forget about his dagger, where was his sabre? His sabre, unfortunately, was on the other side of the sepoy (it was a good thing he had not noticed it because it was so sharp that he would have been able to slice Fleury in two without even pressing). Fleury had no time to draw his final weapon, the two-bladed Indian dagger, for his adversary, it turned out, was no less impressively armed than he was himself and he was already flourishing a spare sabre which he had been carrying for just such an emergency.

In desperation Fleury leapt for the chandelier, with the intention of swinging on it and kicking the sepoy in the face. But the

[163]

chandelier declined to bear his weight and instead of swinging, he merely sat down heavily on the floor in a hail of diamonds and plaster. But as the sepoy lunged forward to put an end to the struggle he stumbled, blinded by the dust and plaster from the ceiling, and fetched up choking on the floor beside Fleury. Fleury again rolled away, tugging at first one dagger, then the other. But both of them refused to yield. His opponent was clumsily getting to his feet as Fleury snatched a violin from a rack of worm-eaten instruments (the survivors of an attempt by the Collector to start a symphony orchestra in the cantonment), snapped it over his knee and leapt on to the sepoy's back, at the same time whipping the violin strings tightly round the sepoy's neck and dragging on them like reins.

The sepoy was a large and powerful man, Fleury had been weakened by the siege; the sepoy had led a hard life of physical combat, Fleury had led the life of a poet, cultivating his sensibilities rather than his muscles and grappling only with sonnets and suchlike . . . But Fleury knew that his life depended on not being shaken off and so he clung on with all his might, his legs gripping the sepoy's waist as tight as a corset, his hands dragging on the two broken pieces of violin. The sepoy staggered off, clutching at the violin strings, out of the music room and down the corridor with Fleury still on his back. He tried to batter his rider against the wall, scrape him off against a fragment of the banisters, but still Fleury held on. They galloped up and down the corridor, blundering into walls and against doors, but still Fleury held on. The man's face had turned black, his eyes were bulging, and at last he crashed to the ground, with such force that he almost shook Fleury off . . . but Fleury remained dragging on the violin until he was certain the sepoy was dead. Then he returned, quaking, to the music-room to collect his sabre. But he was shaking so badly that he had to sit down and have a rest. 'Thank heaven for that violin,' he thought. 'Still, I'd better not stay long with the sepoys attacking . . .' He thought he had better leave the pistol where it was; it was much too heavy to carry around if it was not going to work. He had scarcely made this decision when he looked up. The sepoy was standing there again.

Was he a spectre returning to haunt Fleury? No, unfortunately he was not. The sepoy was no phantasm . . . on the contrary, he looked more consistent than ever. He even had red welts around his throat where the violin strings had been choking him. Moreover, he was chuckling and making humorous observations to Fleury in Hindustani, his eyes gleaming as black as anthracite, pointing at his neck occasionally and shaking his head, as if over an unusually successful jest. Fleury made a dash for his sabre, but the sepoy was much nearer to it and picked it up, making as if to hand it to Fleury, and chuckling more loudly than ever. Fleury faltered backwards as the sepoy advanced, still making as if to offer him the sabre. Fleury tripped over something and sat down on the floor while the sepoy worked his shoulders a little to loosen himself up for a swipe. Fleury thought of jumping out of the window, but it was too high . . . besides, a thousand sepoys were waiting below. The object he had tripped over was the pistol; it was so heavy that it was all he could do to raise it. But when he pulled the trigger, it fired. Indeed, not just one barrel fired, but all fifteen; they were not supposed to, but that was what happened. He found himself confronted now by a midriff and a pair of legs; the wall behind the legs was draped in scarlet. The top half of the sepoy had vanished. So it seemed to Fleury in his excitement, anyway.

from *The Great Mutiny* by Christopher Hibbert (1978)

At the Satichaura Ghat in Cawnpore, the women and children who had survived the massacre, about 125 of them, were pulled out of the river and collected together on the sand by some of the Nana's men. Most were barefoot; many were wounded; some,

[165]

who had pieces of jewellery snatched from them, had bleeding fingers and ears. Once they were all assembled orders were given to molest them no more. They were allowed to accept the skin bags offered to them by a party of water-carriers whose pity was aroused by their plight.

'Their clothes had blood on them,' testified a witness of their removal to the Savada House where Nana Sahib had had his headquarters. 'Two were badly hurt and had their heads bound up with handkerchiefs. Some were . . . covered with mud . . . Some had their dresses torn . . . There were no men in the party, but only some boys of twelve or thirteen years of age.'

The women and children were then taken to the Savada House, and thence to a smaller house near by, a house originally built by a British officer for his mistress and known as Bibighar. Here, on 10 July, they were joined by some officers' wives who had escaped from Fatehgarh and had been captured at Nawabganj. The proposal to kill the hostages seems to have been strongly condemned by the women of Nana Sahib's household who threatened to throw themselves out of a high window if any further murders were committed and who, in the meantime, refused all food and drink.

Despite their protestations, however, the execution of all the hostages was decided upon. First three Englishmen from Fatehgarh, who had been placed in the house a few days previously, together with the merchant Greenway, Greenway's son, and a boy of fourteen, were brought out and shot dead by a squad of sepoys. Then it was announced that the women would also be shot. But the sepoy guard protested; they would not kill the memsahibs. And when the order came to shoot the prisoners, they appear to have put their muskets through the windows of the various rooms and fired them into the ceilings. Exasperated by their behaviour, 'the Begum' went to fetch some less fastidious men who would not shrink from the necessary task of executing Christians. She returned with five, two Hindu peasants, two Mohammedan butchers, and a man wearing the red uniform of

Nana Sahib's bodyguard who was said to be her lover. These men entered the house from which shrieks of terror and screams of pain were presently heard. One of the butchers came out with a broken sword, went over to the hotel and returned with a new one. By nightfall the screaming had stopped but groans continued long after the executioners had left and the doors had been closed.

'The hotel where Nana had his quarters was within fifty yards of this house,' J. W. Sherer wrote in his official report, 'and I am credibly informed that he ordered a nautch and passed the evening with singing and dancing. Early next morning orders were given for the Beebeegurgh to be cleared.'

[Beebeeburgh is the phoneticised pronunciation of Bibighar.]

Daphne Manners describes the Bibighar Gardens, in *The Raj Quartet* (1966).

The Taj Mahal is 'typically Indian', isn't it? Picture-book Moghul stuff. But what makes you give out to it emotionally is the feeling of a man's worship of his wife, which is neither Indian nor un-Indian, but a general human emotion, expressed in this case in an 'Indian' way. This is what I got from the Bibighar. It was a place in which you sensed something having gone badly wrong at one time that hadn't yet been put right but could be if only you knew how. That's the sort of thing you could imagine about any place, but imagining it there, feeling that it was still alive, I said, 'How Indian,' because it was the first place in Mayapore that hit me in this way, and the surprise of being hit made me think I'd come across something typical when all the time it was typical of no place, but only of human acts and desires that leave their mark in the most unexpected and sometimes chilling way.

[167]

from *The Discovery of India* by Jawaharlal Nehru (1946)

British memorials of the Mutiny have been put up in Cawnpore and elsewhere. There is no memorial for the Indians who died. The rebel Indians sometimes indulged in cruel and barbarous behavior; they were unorganized, suppressed, and often angered by reports of British excesses. But there is another side to the picture also, that impressed itself on the mind of India, and in my own province especially the memory of it persists in town and village. One would like to forget all this, for it is a ghastly and horrible picture showing man at his worst, even according to the new standards of barbarity set up by nazism and modern war. But it can only be forgotten, or remembered in a detached, impersonal way when it becomes truly the past with nothing to connect it with the present.

The Miracle of Purun Dass

The Miracle of Purun Dass from *The Second Jungle Book*
by R. Kipling (1895)

In this story, the Indian and English cultures come into very simple, clear focus. If you were to read only one extract from this book this should be it.

There was once a man in India who was Prime Minister of one of the semi-independent native States in the north-western part of the country. He was a Brahmin, so high-caste that caste ceased to have any particular meaning for him; and his father had been an important official in the gay-coloured tag-rag and bobtail of an old-fashioned Hindu Court. But as Purun Dass grew up he felt that the old order of things was changing, and that if any one wished to get on in the world he must stand well with the English, and imitate all that the English believed to be good. At the same time a native official must keep his own master's favour. This was a difficult game, but the quiet, close-mouthed young Brahmin, helped by a good English education at a Bombay University, played it coolly, and rose, step by step, to be Prime Minister of the kingdom. That is to say, he held more real power than his master the Maharajah.

When the old king – who was suspicious of the English, their railways and telegraphs – died, Purun Dass stood high with his young successor, who had been tutored by an Englishman; and between them, though he always took care that his master should have the credit, they established schools for little girls, made roads, and started State dispensaries and shows of agricultural implements, and published a yearly blue-book on the 'Moral and Material Progress of the State', and the Foreign Office and the Government of India were delighted. Very few native States take up English progress altogether, for they will not believe, as Purun Dass showed he did, that what was good for the Englishman must be twice as good for the Asiatic. The Prime Minister became the

[171]

honoured friend of Viceroys, and Governors, and Lieutenant-Governors.

At last he went to England on a visit, and had to pay enormous sums to the priests when he came back; for even so high-caste a Brahmin as Purun Dass lost caste by crossing the black sea. In London he met and talked with every one worth knowing – men whose names go all over the world – and saw a great deal more than he said. He was given honorary degrees by learned universities, and he made speeches and talked of Hindu social reform to English ladies in evening dress, till all London cried, 'This is the most fascinating man we have ever met at dinner since cloths were first laid.'

When he returned to India there was a blaze of glory, for the Viceroy himself made a special visit to confer upon the Maharajah the Grand Cross of the Star of India – all diamonds and ribbons and enamel; and at the same ceremony, while the cannon boomed, Purun Dass was made a Knight Commander of the Order of the Indian Empire; so that his name stood Sir Purun Dass, KCIE.

That evening, at dinner in the big Viceregal tent, he stood up with the badge and collar of the Order on his breast, and replying to the toast of his master's health, made a speech few Englishmen could have bettered.

Next month, when the city had returned to its sun-baked quiet, he did a thing no Englishman would have dreamed of doing; for, so far as the world's affairs went, he died. The jewelled order of his Knighthood went back to the Indian Government, and a new Prime Minister was appointed to the charge of affairs, and a great game of General Post began in all the subordinate appointments. The priests knew what had happened, and the people guessed; but India is the one place in the world where a man can do as he pleases and nobody asks why; and the fact that Dewan Sir Purun Dass, KCIE had resigned position, palace and power, and taken up the begging-bowl and ochre-coloured dress of a Sunnyasi, or holy man, was considered nothing extraordinary. He had been, as the Old Law recommends, twenty years a youth, twenty years a fighter, – though he had never carried a weapon in his life – and twenty years head of a household. He had used his wealth and his power for what he knew both to be worth; he had taken honour when it came his way; he had seen men and cities far and near, and men and cities had stood up and honoured him. Now he would let those things go, as a man drops the cloak he no longer needs.

Behind him, as he walked through the city gates, an antelope skin and brass-handled crutch under his arm, and a begging-bowl of polished brown coco-de-mer in his hand, barefoot, alone, with eyes cast on the ground – behind him they were firing salutes from the bastions in honour of his happy successor. Purun Dass nodded. All that life was ended; and he bore it no more ill-will or good-will than a man bears to a colourless dream of the night. He was a Sunnyasi – a houseless, wandering mendicant, depending on his neighbours for his daily bread; and so long as there is a morsel to divide in India, neither priest nor beggar starves. He had never in his life tasted meat, and very seldom eaten even fish. A five-pound note would have covered his personal expenses for food through any one of the many years in which he had been absolute master of millions of money. Even when he was being lionised in London he had held before him his dream of peace and quiet – the long, white, dusty Indian road, printed all over with bare feet, the incessant, slow-moving traffic, and the sharp-smelling wood smoke curling up under the fig-trees in the twilight, where the wayfarers sit at their evening meal.

Purun Dass

There is a haunting quality about this story, and Purun Dass's alarmingly simple decision. He sees and experiences two worlds, and chooses what must to us seem the least likely, although I think we feel its charm strongly – something that we owe to Kipling's skill. What Kipling implies is that Purun Dass is journeying further towards self-knowledge, prior to the ultimately lonely journey of death. For me, his decision to abandon all forms of material comfort, and set off on his own in order to find and face himself, is a decision that epitomises the power of India. I believe India's so-called spiritual powers are very much to do with discoveries of self-knowledge.

This country can be all things to all people; as Kipling writes, 'India is the one place in the world where a man can do as he pleases and nobody asks why.' The reputation India has acquired as a spiritual home in itself helps people who are searching for one: their minds are open before they even get there. It can provide an apparently uncluttered, simple way of life; there are fewer distractions; things work more slowly; there is more space, and above all, there is time. If you can find time to think, you can find yourself.

Departures

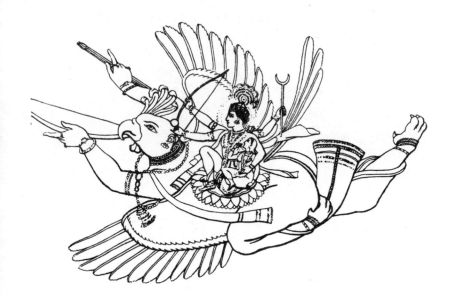

Thinking about sense-objects
Will attach you to sense-objects;
Grow attached and you become addicted;
Thwart your addiction, it turns to anger;
Be angry and you confuse your mind;
Confuse your mind, you forget the lesson of experience;
Forget experience, you lose discrimination;
Lose discrimination, and you miss life's only purpose.

Bhagavad Gita (*c.* 500 BC)

Winston Churchill

It is alarming and also nauseating to see Mr Gandhi, a seditious Middle Temple lawyer, now posing as a fakir of a type well-known in the East, striding half-naked up the steps of the Viceregal palace, while he is still organising and conducting a defiant campaign of civil disobedience, to parley on equal terms with the representative of the King Emperor.

Bengal by Alan Ross (1973)

Against the betel-stained violence
The senseless murders that appal
The oppression of words and climate
That breathe Bengal

You must set the softness of heart,
A querulous literacy,
And the old ox-eyed gentleness
That rips them apart.

from Ken Taylor's adaptation of *The Raj Quartet*

Barbie, the retired missionary, goes into her companion's bedroom softly, supposing her to be asleep, to remove Mabel's glasses, smooth down her bed-clothes and put out the light. Mabel is not asleep, however, so Barbie plucks up the courage to speak to her . . .

She looks down at her friend . . .

BARBIE: Mabel.
MABEL: Yes?
BARBIE: Who is Gillian Waller?
MABEL: Gillian Waller?
BARBIE: Sometimes you say it in your sleep.
MABEL: Jallianwallah. Jallianwallah Bagh. It's not a person. It's a place. The Amritsar Massacre in 1919, where General Dyer killed all those unarmed Indians.
BARBIE: Was your husband there?
MABEL: He died in 1917.
BARBIE: But you remember it?
MABEL: Oh yes, Barbie. £26,000 they raised for General Dyer when they retired him. So I sent £100 to the funds the Indians were raising for the families of their dead. There were more than 260 victims, you see, and £26,000 for him. So I thought £100 was the price of one dead brown.

It's not you, Barbie, and not this house. Jallianwallah Bagh. I gave it to the Indians. That's what she can't forgive. The daughter of the regiment. I'm ready for the light now.

from *India Brittanica* by Geoffrey Moorhouse (1983)

Dyer

In the Punjab in 1919, riots broke out, and a Miss Marcia Sherwood was assaulted by a mob. She was a doctor who had worked for fifteen years in Amritsar, and she had been riding her bicycle down a street when a gang of youths shouting nationalist slogans knocked her to the ground and beat her there until they thought she was dead. She survived because a Hindu family dragged her into their home, treated her injuries, and then smuggled her at night into British hands. By then, reinforcements had been summoned, and Brigadier-General Reginald Dyer came to take up the Amritsar military command.

Dyer was an ailing old sweat, suffering from arterio-sclerosis, and the bronchial effects of chain-smoking. Ill-health had kept him out of the First World War, but he had distinguished himself as a young officer up on the frontier, though even then he had been known as a man with a short temper who was likely to over-react under pressure. He was to do so again in Amritsar with the most terrible consequences. His first act was to proclaim that all further meetings were prohibited, but in spite of this announcement, hordes of people were reported to be gathering on Sunday April 13th, as pilgrims poured into Amritsar for Basakhi Day, one of the most important festivals in the Sikh calendar.

That afternoon thousands were crammed into the Jallianwallah Bagh, a piece of waste-ground popular among travellers as a rendez-vous and resting-place, virtually surrounded by high walls, with access through a narrow alley.

Dyer personally led some troops to this place – all Indians, apart from one other British officer and an NCO – with a couple of armoured cars bringing up the rear. The cars were too wide to be driven through the alley into the Bagh, and remained outside, while fifty riflemen and forty Ghurkas armed only with kukris, entered at the double, their commander marching purposely behind. He gave the crowd no warning. He simply ordered his riflemen to open fire. And when precisely 1,650 rounds of .303 ammunition has been expended, he ordered them to stop; then to about-turn and withdraw; which they did, marching with their rifles at the slope, leaving behind panic, and an uncounted number of wounded; and a death-toll which was officially put at 379 later on, but which Indian sources reckoned at anything between 500 and 1,000.

The Taj Express by Alan Ross (1973)

1

Night expresses hooting across India,
The clank and shunt of an empire

Outstaying its welcome. I open eyes
To an ayah's eyes, the shuffle of cards.

Coaldust on my tongue like a wafer,
And in a swaying lavatory a woman's

Knees slanting moonlight at her belly.
The engines hiss and spill.

The Deccan moored to huge mango trees,
Mosquito nets like child brides.

Stations are marble dormitories, fruitstalls
Inset like altars, wax dripping –

An air of the morgue, all these sleepers
Huddled like mailbags without addresses.

Dawn of papaya and fresh lime.

2

The burra-sahib dressed as for the golfcourse,
Shorts, suede shoes, sports shirt open at the neck.

Outside, the bearer chews *pan* and betel,
Mouth smeared on the edge of haemorrhage.

Whisky and crime stories, and at halts wreaths
Of tuberoses and marigold, ash ceremonies.

Bottles in a dressing case gaudy as spices
In Bow Bazaar, crushed essences like shut parasols.

The rattle of points and bangles. The air
Is sulphurous, spiralling out of mutiny,

The embrace of miners and goddesses,
Where everything escapes, hands palm upward.

from *Farewell the Trumpets* by James Morris (1978)

In London the India Independence Bill ran through all its Parliamentary stages in a single week, ending at a stroke all British claims to sovereignty in India, and abrogating all the hundreds of treaties concluded between the Crown and the Princely States. Mountbatten kept a large calendar on his desk, to mark off the days, like the count-down of a space launching, and with hectic resolution the British in India prepared the obsequies of their paramountcy. It had taken them centuries to pacify and survey the immense expanses of their Indian territories, father succeeding son in the great task: now in a matter of weeks a boundary commission sliced the edifice into parts, laying new frontiers like string on a building-site, under the dispassionate instructions of an English barrister, Sir Cyril Radcliffe, who had never set foot in India before. The Indian Army was bisected, regiments split by squadrons, companies that had served together for a century suddenly distributed among alien battalions. The white Viceregal train chuffed away from Delhi for the last time, for it was allotted to Pakistan: the officials of the Kennel Club were relieved to be told that its assets would remain in India.

from *India Brittanica* by Geoffrey Moorhouse (1983)

All over the subcontinent, the British were packing up to go home. In Lucknow, some sappers hauled down the Union Jack

[181]

from the flagstaff on top of the ruined old Residency, where by special decree it had flown day and night since the mutiny; then they demolished the staff itself and filled up its base with cement, so that nobody else's flag should fly over that poignant place.

Staying On by Paul Scott (1977)

I remember the ceremony we had here in Pankot on Independence eve very clearly still.

At sundown, they beat the retreat. After that we dined at Flagstaff House. Then we went back to the parade ground, and there was a band – a pretty scratch affair. They played all the traditional martial British music. Then there were some Indian pipers, and a Scottish pipe-major. One by one all the floodlights were put out, leaving just the flagpole lit with the Union Jack flying from it. Colonel Layton and the new Indian colonel stood at attention side by side. Then the band played 'Abide with me'.

It was so moving that I began to cry. And Tusker put his hand on mine and kept it there all through the hymn and when we were standing all through 'God Save the King', and all through that terrible lovely moment when the Jack was hauled down inch by inch in utter, utter silence. The only sounds you could hear were the jackals hunting in the hills and the strange little rustles when a gust of wind sent papers and programmes scattering. There was no sound otherwise until on the stroke of midnight the Indian flag began to go up, again very slowly, and then the band began to play the new Indian National Anthem and all the crowds out there in the dark began to sing the words. And when the flag was up there flying and the anthem was finished you never heard such cheering and clapping. I couldn't clap because Tusker still had hold of my hand and didn't let go until all the floodlights came on again and the troops marched off to the sound of the band.

Many stories of the dreadful time of partition can be found in history books, but something of the awful, nightmare quality of the last weeks before Independence are captured for me in this extract.

from *Midnight's Children* by Salman Rushdie (1981)

The main character, Saleem, sits with his son, Aadam: they are about to watch a snake-charming competition . . .

A single shaft of light spilled into a pool on the floor of the Midnight-Confidential Club. From the shadows beyond the fringe of the illuminated area, Aadam and I saw Picture Singh sitting stiffly, cross-legged, next to a handsome Brylcreemed youth; each of them was surrounded by musical instruments and the closed baskets of their art. A loudspeaker announced the beginning of that legendary contest for the title of Most Charming Man In The World; but who was listening? Did anyone even pay attention, or were they too busy with lips tongues hands? This was the name of Pictureji's opponent: the Maharaja of Cooch Naheen.

How long, in that sunless cavern, did they struggle? Months, years, centuries? I cannot say: I watched, mesmerized, as they strove to outdo one another, charming every kind of snake imaginable, asking for rare varieties to be sent from the Bombay snake-farm; and the Maharaja matched Picture Singh snake for snake, succeeding even in charming constrictors, which only Pictureji had previously managed to do. In that infernal Club whose darkness was another aspect of its proprietor's obsession with the colour black (under whose influence he tanned his skin darker darker every day at the Sun 'n' Sand), the two virtuosi goaded snakes into impossible feats, making them tie themselves

[183]

in knots, or bows, or persuading them to drink water from wine-glasses, and to jump through fiery hoops . . . defying fatigue, hunger and age, Picture Singh was putting on the show of his life (but was anyone looking? Anyone at all?) – and at last it became clear that the younger man was tiring first; his snakes ceased to dance in time to his flute; and finally, through a piece of sleight-of-hand so fast that I did not see what happened, Picture Singh managed to knot a king cobra around the Maharaja's neck.

What Picture said: 'Give me best, captain, or I'll tell it to bite.'

That was the end of the contest. The humiliated princeling left the Club and was later reported to have shot himself in a taxi. And on the floor of his last great battle, Picture Singh collapsed like a falling banyan tree . . . blind attendants (to one of whom I entrusted Aadam) helped me carry him from the field.

from *The Discovery of India* by Jawaharlal Nehru (1946)

As I grew up and became engaged in activities which promised to lead to India's freedom, I became obsessed with the thought of India. What was this India that possessed me and beckoned to me continually, urging me to action so that we might realize some vague but deeply felt desire of our hearts? The initial urge came to me, I suppose, through pride, both individual and national, and the desire, common to all men, to resist another's domination and have freedom to live the life of our choice. It seemed monstrous to me that a great country like India, with a rich and immemorial past, should be bound hand and foot to a faraway island which imposed its will upon her. It was still more monstrous that this forcible union had resulted in poverty and degradation beyond measure. That was reason enough for me and for others to act.

But it was not enough to satisfy the questioning that arose

within me. What is this India, apart from her physical and geographical aspects? What did she represent in the past; what gave strength to her then? How did she lose that old strength, and has she lost it completely? Does she represent anything vital now, apart from being the home of a vast number of human beings? How does she fit in to the modern world?

from the diary . . .

On our last night in Udaipur, I went from the temple, to say good-bye to Narendra Singh. His eleven year old house-boy Kooba, whom Narendra had taken on at the request of a poor father unable to care for thirteen children, showed me the little outhouse by the gate where he slept. He liked the cramped little shed and the sack-cloth bedding which was all that came between him and the bare earth. I could have coped with everything except his pride; but this Western sentimentalism is out of place in the face of poverty in the East, and Kooba, after all, enjoyed a relatively privileged life.

I did not want to leave Narendra's. When I did tear myself away, and say good-bye, all he said was, 'There is no good-bye. You will come again'.

I had a lift back into town on the back of a motor-scooter: there were three of us squashed on to it. I collected my bike, and rode back to the hotel, dodging a barking dog who leapt at me from a shadowed doorway, avoiding the cows sleeping in the ill-lit streets: I could hear them breathing before I could see them.

Who should I see back at the hotel, but B.J. laying breakfast for the morning. I went into the dining-room to say good-bye. He looked up, put down his fistful of cutlery and ran across the

[185]

room, throwing his arms around me! It was more than a little unexpected. He had tears in his eyes.

'Goodbye shir. Oh goodbye' he said, 'I never forget you.'

'Good-bye B.J., I shall never forget you,' I croaked. He still had his arms around me.

'I shee you again in the morning when you leave, shir, and shay goodbye.'

'Please don't get up specially, B.J. We're off very early.'

'Oh yesh, shir. I will be there.'

The coach left at 6.30 a.m. and there were plenty of people to see us off – there seemed to be twice as many staff as usual, all eager for a decent tip – but there was one face I wanted to see, and didn't. B.J. was not there.

It was a clear morning. The sun was rising, and the moon was setting over the hills beyond the lake in front of the hotel. The coach pulled away and began rolling down the sloping drive. I was very upset by leaving, lost in memories of Udaipur and its people; and of the excitement of our work there. I felt let down by B.J.; words, I thought to myself, just words. Geraldine tapped me on the shoulder.

'Look', she said. She pointed to the road, fifty yards below us, and there, wrapped in their shawls against the morning chill, slowly waving good-bye, were B.J. and his wife, with their son and daughter. Once again I had to fight back the tears.

I learned much later, that B.J. had asked Charlie to take his daughter back to England with him – 'to lead a better life'.

from the diary . . .

My last night in Simla: shortly before my return to England.

A feeling of relief that I had completed my location filming, combined with a sense of impending loss, for I was soon to be leaving India, tinged my final walk through the town.

I wanted to photograph something I had seen on an earlier walk when I had not had my camera with me, and I wandered along the maze of alleys, and up and down steps in the chill dusk, trying to find it. Beneath the ramshackle corrugated iron rooves that cluttered the curving slope of the hill, people were lighting their evening fires. Smoke drifted lazily up from chimnies, and as it rose above the shadow of the hill it caught the rays of the dying sun. The smell of burning pine incensed the air. Lights were lit in the bazaar, and in the windows of the houses higher up, lending the hill the aspect of the night-sky above it, as it too, began to fill with stars. I continued to search, frustrated by not being able to find what I was looking for . . .

What I had seen on my earlier ramblings was a door, and by it, a bell with a label. The label bore, quite simply, the name 'Kumar'. Underneath, it said something like 'Teller of Oaths'. I was stunned: it was as though Hari Kumar himself had come to life, left the pages of the books we were filming, and come to live in Simla: I felt a kind of duty to relocate him.

On this, the night of our departure, it was 'Kumar' I was looking for; it was strangely like Guy Perron, searching for Hari: Coomer, Kumar – one man swallowed by the huge tide of Anglo-Indian history. But of course Kumar will never be found, which is why he haunts me; and my search – like Perron's – was fruitless.

Death

If I am to die by the bullet
of a madman,
I must do so smiling.
There must be
no anger within me.
God must be
in my heart and on my lips.
And you promise me
one thing.
Should such a thing happen,
you are not to shed one tear.

Ghandi, January 28th 1940

from *Portrait of India* by Ved Mehta (1970)

Srinagar (1966)

Clear water, soft sun in a late afternoon sky, mountains that seem close, steep. I've just hired a shikara – a kind of gondola. I lie back and allow myself to be lulled by the gentle rocking-motion.

'Sahib like full tour dahl lake?' The shikara wallah asks, in pidgin English.

He propels the shikara with little heart-shaped oars. 'Sahib is first tourist this year. Tourists staying away from Kashmir these days. Very troubled times. Sahib will give Kashmir happy fortune.'

He has left off his rowing and edged around to the stern, where he prepares tea over open coals. He serves it to me from an urn.

'We reach Nagin Lake in two hours. If Sahib is lucky, Sahib will meet flower-wallah Bulbul. If Sahib likes, he'll sing native Kashmiri song telling of the affair of the bumble bee and the tulip. Every day he rending heart-singing song on Nagin lake.'

We drift past 'Princess Margaret', 'Churchill'. On a deck verandah, an elderly English lady wearing a lace fichu is sunning herself, drinking tea, watching swans and kingfishers dive and paddle around her houseboat. Silver service, crumpets, scones. A Memsahib to her toes. I imagine she came here some time after the First World War, loved the place, and settled down with a retinue of houseboys. I imagine her thinking, 'Yes, some things have changed. But in things that count, all is as it used to be. Slightly fewer friends perhaps'.

I must launch out my boat by Rabindraneth Tagore (1936)

I must launch out my boat. The languid hours
Pass by on the shore – alas for me!
The spring has done its flowering and taken leave.
And now with the burden of faded futile flowers I wait
    and linger.
The waves have become clamorous, and upon the bank
In the shady lane the yellow leaves flutter and fall.
What emptiness do you gaze upon! Do you not feel
A thrill passing through the air with the notes of
The far away song floating from the other shore?

from the *Katha Upanishad* (800–400 BC)

Nachiketas questions death

NACHIKETAS: When a man dies, this doubt arises: some say 'he is', some say 'he is not'. Teach me the truth.

DEATH: Take horses and gold and elephants: choose sons and grandsons that shall live a hundred years. Have vast expanses of land, and live as many years as you desire. To attend on you I will give you fair maidens with chariots and musical instruments. But ask me not, Nachiketas, the secrets of death.

NACHIKETAS: All these pleasures pass away. They weaken the power of life. Grant me the gift that unveils the mystery. Solve the doubt as to the great beyond. This is the one gift Nachiketas can ask. 'Solve the doubt as to the great beyond.'

[192]

Perhaps you remember the incident in the Bibighar, during the Indian Mutiny (see 'Bonds of Hatred'), when many English were butchered. It was of course a warning that a people can not be held in suppression indefinitely before they seek freedom, or even revenge.

from *The Raj Quartet* by Paul Scott (1975)

He took me into Merrick's bedroom. What I expected was just the sight of Merrick dead in bed but the whole place was an absolute shambles. The mosquito net was ripped to ribbons, the bedsheets were all over the place and stained with blood and Merrick was lying on the floor, dressed in his Pathan clothes, but hacked about with his own ornamental axe and strangled with his own sash. And all over the floor there were chalked cabalistic signs. And someone had scrawled the word Bibighar across Susan's dressing-table mirror with the same brown make-up stick that had been used to daub his face.

from *Freedom at Midnight* by Lapierre and Collins (1981)

The Punjab, just after Independence

Boota Singh, a 55-year-old Sikh veteran of Mountbatten's Burma campaign, was working his fields one September afternoon when he heard a terrified scream behind him. He turned to see a young girl, pursued by a fellow Sikh, rushing towards him. The girl threw herself at Boota Singh, begging 'Save me, save me!'

He stepped between the girl and her captor. He understood instantly what had happened. The girl was a Moslem whom the Sikh had seized from a passing refugee column. This wholly unexpected intrusion of the province's miseries upon his plot of

[193]

land offered Boota Singh a providential opportunity to resolve the problem most oppressing him, his own solitude. He was a shy man who'd never married, first because of his family's inability to purchase him a wife, then because of his natural timidity.

'How much?' he asked the girl's captor.

'Fifteen hundred rupees,' was the answer.

Boota Singh did not even bargain. He went into his hut and returned with a soiled pile of rupee notes. The girl whom those banknotes purchased was 17 years old, thirty-eight years his junior. Her name was Zenib.

To the lonely old Sikh she became an adorable plaything, half daughter, half mistress, a wondrous presence who completely disrupted his life. The affection he'd never been able to bestow burst over Zenib in a floodtide.

To Zenib, who'd been beaten and raped before her flight, the compassion and tenderness poured out to her by the lonely old Sikh was as overwhelming as it was unexpected. Inevitably, her response was grateful affection and she quickly became the pole around which Boota Singh's life turned.

One day that autumn, well before the dawn as Sikh tradition dictated, a strange melody of flutes advanced down the road to Boota Singh's house. Surrounded by singers and neighbours carrying sputtering torches, astride a horse harnessed in velvet and bangles, Boota Singh rode up to the doorstep of his own home to claim as his bride the little moslem girl he'd purchased with a soiled stack of rupee notes.

A few weeks later the season which had brought so much horror and hardship to his fellow Punjabis bestowed a last gift on Boota Singh. His wife announced she was bearing the heir he'd despaired of ever having – a baby girl. Following Sikh custom, Boota Singh opened the Sikh Holy Book, the *Granth Sahib*, at random and gave his daughter a name beginning with the first letter of the word he found at the top of the page. The letter was a 'T' and he chose Tanveer – Miracle of the Sky.

Several years later, a pair of Boota Singh's nephews, furious at losing a chance to inherit his property, reported Zenib's presence to the authorities who were trying to locate women abducted during the exodus. Zenib was wrenched from Boota Singh and placed in a camp while efforts were made to locate her family in Pakistan.

Desperate, Boota Singh rushed to New Delhi and accomplished at the Grand Mosque the most difficult act a Sikh could perform. He cut his hair and became a Moslem. Re-named Jamil Ahmed, Boota Singh presented himself at the office of Pakistan's High Commissioner and demanded the return of his wife. It was a useless gesture. The two nations had agreed that implacable rules would govern the exchange of abducted women: married or not, they would be returned to the families from which they had been forcibly separated.

For six months Boota Singh visited his wife daily in the detention camp. He would sit beside her in silence, weeping for their lost dream of happiness. Finally, he learned her family had been located. The couple embraced in a tearful farewell, Zenib vowing never to forget him and to return to him and their daughter as soon as she could.

The desperate Boota Singh applied for the right as a Moslem to immigrate to Pakistan. His application was refused. He applied for a visa. That too was refused. Finally, taking with him his daughter, renamed Sultana, he crossed the frontier illegally. Leaving the girl in Lahore, he made his way to the village where Zenib's family had settled. There he received a cruel shock. His wife had been remarried with a cousin only hours after the truck bringing her back from India had deposited her in the village. The poor man, weeping 'give me back my wife', was brutally beaten by Zenib's brothers and cousins, then handed over to the police as an illegal immigrant.

Brought to trial, Boota Singh pleaded he was a Moslem and begged the judge to return his wife to him. If only, he said, he could be granted the right to see his wife, to ask her if she would return to India with him and their daughter, he would be satisfied.

[195]

Moved by his plea, the judge agreed. The confrontation took place a week later in a courtroom overflowing with spectators alerted by newspaper reports of the case. A terrified Zenib, escorted by an angry and possessive horde of her relatives, was brought into the chamber. The judge indicated Boota Singh.

'Do you know this man?' he asked.

'Yes,' replied the trembling girl, 'he's Boota Singh, my first husband.' Then Zenib identified her daughter standing by the elderly Sikh.

'Do you wish to return with them to India?' the judge asked. Boota Singh turned his pleading eyes on the young girl who had brought so much happiness to his life. Behind Zenib, other eyes fixed on her quivering figure, a battery glaring at her from the audience, the male members of her clan warning her against trying to renounce the call of her blood. An atrocious tension gripped the courtroom. His lined face alive with a desperate hope, Boota Singh watched Zenib's lips, waiting for the favourable reply he was sure would come. For an unbearably long moment the room was silent.

Zenib shook her head. 'No,' she whispered.

A gasp of anguish escaped Boota Singh. He staggered back against the railing behind him. When he'd regained his poise, he took his daughter by the hand and crossed the room.

'I cannot deprive you of your daughter, Zenib,' he said. 'I leave her to you.' He took a clump of bills from his pocket and offered them to his wife, along with their daughter. 'My life is finished now,' he said simply.

The judge asked Zenib if she wished to accept his offer of the custody of their daughter. Again, an agonizing silence filled the courtroom. From their seats Zenib's male relatives furiously shook their heads. They wanted no Sikh blood defiling their little community.

Zenib looked at her daughter with the eyes of despair. To accept her would be to condemn her to a life of misery. An awful sob shook her frame. 'No,' she gasped.

Boota Singh, his eyes overflowing with tears, stood for a long moment looking at his weeping wife, trying perhaps to fix forever in his mind the blurred image of her face. Then he tenderly picked up his daughter and, without turning back, left the courtroom.

The despairing man spent the night weeping and praying in the mausoleum of the Moslem saint Data Gang Baksh, while his daughter slept against a nearby pillar. With the dawn, he took the girl to a nearby bazaar. There, using the rupees he'd tendered to his wife the afternoon before, he bought her a new robe and a pair of sandals embroidered in gold brocade. Then, hand in hand, the old Sikh and his daughter walked to the nearby railroad station of Shahdara. Waiting on the platform for the train to arrive, the weeping Boota Singh explained to his daughter that she would not see her mother again.

In the distance a locomotive's whistle shrieked. Boota Singh tenderly picked up his daughter and kissed her. He walked to the edge of the platform. As the locomotive burst into the station the little girl felt her father's arms tighten around her. Then suddenly she was plunging forward. Boota Singh had leapt into the path of the onrushing locomotive. The girl heard again the roar of the whistle mingled this time with her own screams. Then she was in the blackness beneath the engine.

Boota Singh was killed instantly, but by a miracle his daughter survived unscathed. On the old Sikh's mutilated corpse, the police found a blood-soaked farewell note to the young wife who had rejected him.

'My dear Zenib,' it said, 'you listened to the voice of the multitude, but that voice is never sincere. Still my last wish is to be with you. Please bury me in your village and come from time to time to put a flower on my grave.'

Mother Theresa must be known to most of the readers of this book. Born in Albania, she founded, in 1948, the Catholic 'Missionaries of Charity'. She is now the head of an enormous organisation, helping the sick, the poor, the hungry; she helps education, she aids the dissemination of The Word of God, and ministers to the dying.

from *Mother Teresa: Her People and their Work* by Desmond Doig
(1976)

Of the 'poorest of the poor' she says . . .

They have lived like animals, we help them to die like angels. One poor unfortunate woman was brought in from the sewer. She was a beggar who had, apparently overcome by hunger and fatigue, fallen into an open manhole. She lay there for five days barely alive and covered with maggots. As I put her to bed and began gently cleaning her, whole areas of skin came off in my hand. The woman, half-unconscious, murmured
  'Why are you doing this for me?'
  I replied 'For the love of God'.
  This poor waif who probably never in her life had had loving hands tend her – looking at me, her soul in her eyes, faith in human nature restored – gave me a most beautiful smile and died. That is our reward – that we should make the last moments of the fellow-being beautiful.

from the diary . . .

I became transfixed by some gravestones, nestling under a banyan tree. English graves are very common in India, and children's graves, of course, figure prominently: I later read a book called *Two Monsoons*, so named because if a newly-born baby could be nursed through two monsoons, the chances were that it would survive.

On closer inspection the crosses that I had noticed turned out to be children's graves, and they haunted me. There was something heart-rending about this little cluster of stones marking the deaths of English children, beneath a holy tree in a foreign land.

'There is a corner of a foreign field . . .'

It filled me with an aching sense of nationalism, and at the same time, a profound sense of hollowness and futility.

I found a moving epitaph in *Two Monsoons*, and William Ayot worked these threads into the following passage.

from *Bengal Lancer* (the play)

Further along the road, beyond the jheel lake, stood an ancient banyan tree. Huge tree. Its branches had rooted long ago, forming a vault like the bones of a ruined church. Inside, in its quiet shade, stood a group of crosses, victorian graves. All children. 'Lucy – from the cholera'. 'Georgie from a snake'. 'Amelia Jane. Departed this life the tenth of April 1857. Aged seven months, seven days and one hour'. With the inscription – 'In the morning it was green and growing up. In the evening it was cut and withered like a flower'.

Elegy on a Young Warrior by Ponmutiyar (Second century)

> O heart sorrowing
> for this lad
>   once scared

of a stick
lifted in mock-anger
when he refused
a drink of milk,
       now
not content with killing
war-elephants
with spotted trunks,
       this son
of the strong man who fell yesterday

seems unaware of the arrow
in his wound,
his head of hair is plumed
like a horse's,
       he's fallen
on his shield,
his beard still soft.

Gunga Din by Rudyard Kipling (1898)

You may talk o' gin and beer
When you're quartered safe out 'ere,
An' you're sent to penny-fights an' Aldershot it;
But when it comes to slaughter
You will do your work on water,
An' you'll lick the bloomin' boots of 'im that's got it.
Now in Injia's sunny clime,
Where I used to spend my time
A-servin' of 'Er Majesty the Queen,
Of all them blackfaced crew

The finest man I knew
Was our regimental bhisti, Gunga Din.
   He was 'Din! Din! Din!
  'You limpin' lump o' brick-dust, Gunga Din!
   'Hi! Slippy *hitherao*!
   'Water, get it! *Panee lao*,
  'You squidgy-nosed old idol, Gunga Din.'

The uniform 'e wore
Was nothin' much before,
An' rather less than 'arf o' that be'ind,
For a piece o' twisty rag
An' a goatskin water-bag
Was all the field-equipment 'e could find.
When the sweatin' troop-train lay
In a sidin' through the day,
Where the 'eat would make your bloomin' eyebrows crawl,
We shouted 'Harry By!'
Till our throats were bricky-dry,
Then we wopped 'im 'cause 'e couldn't serve us all.
   It was 'Din! Din! Din!
  'You 'eathen, where the mischief 'ave you been?
   'You put some *juldee* in it
   'Or I'll *marrow* you this minute
  'If you don't fill up my helmet, Gunga Din!'

'E would dot an' carry one
Till the longest day was done;
An' 'e didn't seem to know the use o' fear.
If we charged or broke or cut,
You could bet your bloomin' nut,
'E'd be waitin' fifty paces right flank rear.
With 'is mussick on 'is back,
'E would skip with our attack,
An' watch us till the bugles made 'Retire,'

An' for all 'is dirty 'ide
'E was white, clear white, inside
When 'e went to tend the wounded under fire!
    It was 'Din! Din! Din!'
    With the bullets kickin' dust-spots on the green.
      When the cartridges ran out,
      You could hear the front-ranks shout,
    'Hi! ammunition-mules an' Gunga Din!'

I shan't forgit the night
When I dropped be'ind the fight
With a bullet where my belt-plate should 'a' been.
I was chokin' mad with thirst,
An' the man that spied me first
Was our good old grinnin', gruntin' Gunga Din.
'E lifted up my 'ead,
An' he plugged me where I bled,
An' 'e guv me 'arf-a-pint o' water green.
It was crawlin' and it stunk,
But of all the drinks I've drunk,
I'm gratefullest to one from Gunga Din.
    It was 'Din! Din! Din!
  ''Ere's a beggar with a bullet through 'is spleen;
    ''E's chawin' up the ground,
    'An' 'e's kickin' all around:
  'For Gawd's sake git the water, Gunga Din!'

'E carried me away
To where a dooli lay,
An' a bullet come an' drilled the beggar clean.
'E put me safe inside,
An' just before 'e died,
'I 'ope you liked your drink,' sez Gunga Din.
So I'll meet 'im later on
At the place where 'e is gone –

Where it's always double drill and no canteen.
'E'll be squattin' on the coals
Givin' drink to poor damned souls,
An' I'll get a swig in hell from Gunga Din!
  Yes, Din! Din! Din!
 You Lazarushian-leather Gunga Din!
  Though I've belted you and flayed you,
  By the livin' Gawd that made you,
 You're a better man than I am, Gunga Din!

Gandhi

I shall be content to be written down an impostor if my lips utter a
word of anger or abuse against my assailant at the last moment

Gandhi's last Words, January 30th 1948

He Ram
(O God)

Time by Bhartrihari (500 AD)

Time is the root of all this earth;
These creatures who from time had birth,
Within his bosom at the end
Shall sleep; Time hath nor enemy nor friend.

Time hath nor enemy nor friend.

[203]

All we in one long caravan
Are journeying since the world began;
We know not whither, but we know
Time guideth at the front, and all must go.

Time guideth at the front and all must go

Like as the wind upon the field
Bows every herb, and all must yield
So we beneath Time's passing breath
Bow each in turn – Why tears for Birth or Death?

Why tears for Birth or Death?

Reincarnation

from
How to Live in Suburbia
when your Heart is
In the Himalayas
by Gwen Davis

Think of your husband as a lover from an another life,
and wonder what you did to deserve him.

from the *Bhagavad Gita* (*c.* 500 BC)

Some say this Atman
Is slain, and others
Call It the slayer:
They know nothing.
How can It slay
Or who shall slay It?

Know this Atman
Unborn, undying,
Never ceasing,
Never beginning,
Deathless, birthless,
Unchanging for ever.
How can It die
The death of the body?

Knowing It birthless,
Knowing It deathless,
Knowing It endless,
For ever unchanging,
Dream not you do
The deed of the killer,
Dream not the power
Is yours to command it.

Worn-out garments
Are shed by the body:
Worn-out bodies
Are shed by the dweller
Within the body.
New bodies are donned
By the dweller, like garments.

Not wounded by weapons,
Not burned by fire,
Not dried by the wind,
Not wetted by water:
Such is the Atman.

These famous words were spoken by Jawaharlal Nehru, India's
first Prime Minister at Midnight on 14th August, 1947.

'Long years ago we made a tryst with destiny and now the time
comes when we shall redeem our pledge, not wholly or in full
measure, but very substantially.

'At the stroke of the midnight hour, while the world sleeps, India
will awake to life and freedom.

'At the dawn of history India started on her unending quest and
the trackless centuries are filled with her striving, and the gran-
deur of her successes and her failures. Through good and ill
fortunes alike she has never lost sight of that quest or forgotten
the ideal which gave her strength. We end today a period of ill
fortune and India discovers herself again.'

from *Exile* by R. Parthasarathy (1977)

It's a tired sea accosts the visitor
between Fort St George and San Thome.
Here, once, ships bottled the harbour

with spices, cinnamon and cloves.
Inland, an old civilization
hissed in the alleys and wells.

The sun has done its worst:
skimmed a language,
worn it to a shadow.

The eyes ache from feeding too much
on the ripe fruit of temples.
Bridges tame unruly rivers.

The hourglass of the Tamil mind
is replaced by the exact chronometer
of Europe. Now,

cardboard-and-paper goddesses (naturally
high-breasted) look down on Mount Road.
There is no fight left in the old beast.

Time has plucked her teeth. Francis Day*
has seen to that. What have I come
here for from a thousand miles?

The sky is no different.
Beggars are the same everywhere. The clubs
are there, complete with bar and golf-links.

The impact of the West on India
is still talked about,
though the wogs have taken over.

*Agent of the East India Company who built Fort St George which later
became Madras.

[209]

You may recall the old Sikh, Bootah Singh, whose marriage to a young Moslem girl, Zenib, ended so tragically . . .

from *Freedom at Midnight* by Lapierre and Collins (1981)

Boota Singh's suicide stirred a wave of emotion in Pakistan and his funeral became an event of national importance. Even in death, however, the elderly Sikh remained a symbol of those terrible days when the Punjab was in flames. Zenib's family and the inhabitants of their village refused to permit Boota Singh's burial in the village cemetery. The village males, led by Zenib's second husband, barred entrance to his coffin on 22 February 1957.

Rather than provoke a riot, the authorities ordered the coffin and the thousands of Pakistanis touched by Boota Singh's drama who'd followed it to return to Lahore. There, under a mountain of flowers, Boota Singh's remains were interred.

Zenib's family, however, enraged by the honour extended to Boota Singh, sent a commando to Lahore to uproot and profane his tomb. Their savage action provoked a remarkable outburst from the city's population. Boota Singh was re-interred under another mountain of flowers. This time hundreds of Moslems volunteered to guard the grave of the Sikh convert, illustrating by their generous gesture the hope that time might eventually efface in the Punjab the bitter heritage of 1947.

from *The Koran* translated by N. J. Darwood (1956)

When you recite the Koran, We place between you and those who deny the life to come a hidden barrier. We cast a veil upon their hearts and make them hard of hearing, lest they understand it. That is why on hearing mention of your One and Only Lord, they turn their backs in flight.

We well know what they wish to hear when they listen to you, and what they say when they converse in private; when the wrongdoers declare: 'The man you follow is surely bewitched.'

Behold what epithets they bestow upon you. They have surely gone astray and cannot find the right path.

'What!' they say. 'When we are turned to bones and dust, shall we be restored to life?'

Say: 'You shall; whether you turn to stone or iron, or any other substance which you may think unlikely to be given life.'

They will ask: 'Who will restore us?'

Say: 'He that created you at first.'

They will shake their heads and ask: 'When will this be?'

Say: 'It may be near at hand. On that day He will summon you all, and you shall answer Him with praises. You shall think that you have stayed away but for a little while.'

Sawai Man Singh II managed to retain his unique position as the Maharajah of Jaipur even after Independence, steering his people through partition with remarkably few incidents of violence by adopting a humanitarian, widely-based religious view. He celebrated his Silver Jubilee in December 1947, and his subjects were treated to a lavish display of spectacular extravagance. He is referred to in the following extract as 'Jai' – an abbreviation of Jaipur.

from *The Last Maharajah* by Quentin Crewe (1985)

Jai was weighed against silver and the money given to the poor. It being the polo season, he was in good training and so weighed less than he might have done at another time of year. Both his wives were weighed, too, in the privacy of the zenana. The culmination of the festivities was a huge darbar, conducted in full ceremonial dress, to which Lord and Lady Mountbatten came. Mountbatten invested Jai as a Grand Commander of the Star of India. All the other orders of the Indian Empire had been suspended with Independence. For some reason, the Star had not. Mountbatten asked the King if he might give it to two Maharajas who had been most co-operative and helpful in the difficulties over the accession. They were Bikaner and Jaipur – the two who called him by his Christian name.

Jai presented Mountbatten with a jade-handled dagger, bejewelled with rubies and emeralds. It had been captured by Man Singh I in 1585 from an Afghan warrior.

Naturally, the darbar was followed by a polo match. Mountbatten protested that he had not played since before the war and, in any case, had no clothes. Jai had anticipated this excuse and had arranged for some clothes to be made for him. One hundred and thirty six ponies were paraded, from which Mountbatten was to choose six. (Mountbatten, it goes without saying, recorded that he played pretty well.)

In the evening, they went to the opening of a new cinema called The Polo Victory. Jai had given the polo-stick maker who had accompanied him on his famous polo tour of 1933 a plot of land. On it he had built this cinema, named in honour of the tour. They all watched an old film of the victorious team in action. Unfortunately, it was run backwards, but everyone was too polite to mention this.

Routine by Keki Daruwalla (1982)

The putties were left behind by the Raj
a strip of fire round the legs in June.
Within the burning crash-helmet
the brain is a fire-pulp. The asphalt
gives way beneath our boots and sticks.
The edges of the crowd give way;
a ring of abuse re-forms behind us.
We hardly hear them for we are used to it.
Their gamut ranges from 'mother-' to 'sister-seducer'.

Karam Singh marching in the same rank as I
curses under his breath,
'I have children older than them,
these kids whose pubes have hardly sprouted!'

We march to the street-crossing where young blood
fulfils itself by burning tramcars.
Beneath our khaki we are a roasted brown
but unconvinced, they wish to burn our khaki skins.
We are a platoon against a thousand.
It's all well rehearsed; a few words of warning –
a chill formality lost in fiery slogans!
'Load!' I put a piece of death up the spout.
It is well rehearsed: I alone point
my barrel into them as I squeeze the trigger.
The rest aim into the sun!

They have gone. The salvage Squad comes
and takes the body to the autopsy room
and tows the tramcar away.
Tension oozes out as armpits run with sweat.
Depressed and weary we march back to the Lines.
A leader says over the evening wireless,
'We are marching forward.'

from *Very Indian Poems in Indian English* by Nissim Ezekiel
(1982)

The Patriot

I am standing for peace and non-violence.
Why world is fighting fighting
Why all people of world
Are not following Mahatma Gandhi,
I am simply not understanding.
Ancient Indian Wisdom is 100% correct.
I should say even 200% correct.
But Modern generation is neglecting –
Too much going for fashion and foreign thing.

Other day I'm reading in newspaper
(Every day I'm reading Times of India
To improve my English Language)
How one goonda fellow
Throw stone at Indirabehn.
Must be student unrest fellow, I am thinking.
Friends, Romans, Countrymen, I am saying (to myself)
Lend me the ears.
Everything is coming –
Regeneration, Remuneration, Contraception.
Be patiently, brothers and sisters.

You want one glass lassi?
Very good for digestion.
With little salt lovely drink,
Better than wine;
Not that I am ever tasting the wine.
I'm the total teetotaller, completely total.
But I say
Wine is for the drunkards only.

What you think of prospects of world peace?
Pakistan behaving like this,
China behaving like that,
It is making me very sad, I am telling you.
Really, most harassing me.
All men are brothers, no?
In India also
Gujaraties, Maharashtrians, Hindiwallahs
All brothers –
Though some are having funny habits.
Still, you tolerate me,
I tolerate you,
One day Ram Rajya is surely coming.

You are going?
But you will visit again
Any time, any day,
I am not believing in ceremony.
Always I am enjoying your company.

7/1 Burdwan Road, Calcutta by Alan Ross (1981)

The rose he placed in my button-hole –
The son of the son of the old mali,
Who daily, salaaming from his flowerbeds,
Passed just such a rose to my father –

Was that shade of over-florid blue,
Crimson veined by faintest of inkmarks,
I associate with shaving my father's cheek,
As the razor scraped off the lather.

[215]

Seven by one, Burdwan Road,
The address found on an old
Birth certificate. A company house now,
Used by rubber and teak-wallahs,

In from Up Country. Its verandahs
Held chatter of ayahs, squabbles
Between bearers. On the lawn once
A cobra drifted from its sack.

Raj by John Cotton (1975)

Long before the lowering of flags
it was already dying.
In the mess the fading sepia
of polo teams, a subscription
still obligatory
though there were no ponies.

The pipe band on Sundays
and Mozart on records
in the officers' club.

Not far and a stiff climb
the caves where in their darkness
the many armed Shiva
still dances, *Tandava*,
his power surviving
in the universal lingam,

[216]

and a Greek inscription
reminds that others had been before
                    and departed.
As Akbar's Gate of Victory
                    still stands

(he never returning)

> *The world is a bridge*
> *pass over it*
> *but build no house here.*

Elsewhere the town plans of the Indus Valley.

In the city the white caps of Congress
punctuated the crowds
on betel mottled pavements
near somebody else's
Gateway to India,
while sculptured millenial lovers

continued to fondle
their moon-breasted paramours,
and holy bathers
courted cholera and immortality
in that order.

What now remains?
The uniforms, the language
of Shakespeare Wallah
alongside the Vedas,
mother of Sanskrit and
grandmother of languages,

> *who produced it here?*

[217]

the ciphered Victorian pillar-boxes at Ooty
and the English country graveyards.

Yet Shiva too is a haunter of cemeteries.
The past haunting us
as it always haunts the present.

here is another bond to break

But India, as Gandhi insisted,
is to be found in the villages:
in the cool first air of morning,
the jasmine and joss of the bazaar
above which bats hang from the trees
like great leathern fruit,
the cave-ribbed oxen,
the dry-dust roads
and the tenacity to survive
a poverty the West has forgotten.

And carved long before
into the rock of the hillside
Ganeśa,
                    the elephant-headed pathfinder
                    and protector of crossroads,
stands guard
                    as with evening
intruders depart
with the heat of the day
to leave that which endures
to reassert itself.

Awake O Ancient East by Rabindraneth Tagore (1936)

Awake, O ancient East!
The moonless night of the Ages
Has mantled you in its deep gloom.
In your slumber you had vanished in the sea of oblivion.

Awake, O ancient East!
The many-toned melodies of life have ceased,
Like the dying notes of a cricket.
When shall the call of light
Dance again in your pulse?
Awake, O ancient East!

Who shall bring His message?
I am waiting for the moment
When the touchstone of the new dawn
Shall turn this earth to gold.
Awake, O ancient East!

With clasped hands I pray:
Breaking the shackles of old age,
May your new form bloom afresh
In the refulgent glory of the rising sun.
Awake, O ancient East!

The New Age is heralded with the call:
'Open, open the door! let darkness perish,
And lustre, born of sorrow and pain,
Shine forth in you.'
Awake, O ancient East!

from the diary . . .

(At a time when my spirits were quite low in India, when the
filming was being delayed by weather problems and I was ill,
when I felt that all my optimism for real contact with Indians was
destroyed and that the only way to survive was through isolating
oneself from the difficulties of the country and the problems of
mutual understanding in some remote cantonment of the mind,
this small incident reaffirmed my faith in the possibility of a
relationship between our two peoples.)

You may recall Dinesh Sharma from 'Childhood', earlier in this
book.

In the latter days of my stay in Udaipur, I had been upset that
the painting of an elephant that Dinesh had promised me for our
son, Tom, had not been completed before my departure. Most
of the company were agreed that Udaipur – it was two months
since we had left – was the most enjoyable place we had stayed
in, so when Nick le Prevost (who plays Nigel Rowan) asked
us where he should go in India with his time off, we were
unanimous in our decision to send him there. Whilst we
soldiered on against the odds in Simla, Nick went off to
Udaipur: we saw him leave on the little mountain train that runs
from Simla down through the hills to Chandigargh.
   On his return, Nick, who had had a marvellous time, said to
me: 'Oh by the way, Tim. I've got something for you. Bit of a
surprise.' I had no idea what it could be.
   He came to my room that evening to tell me what it was.
   Strolling through the streets of Udaipur, he had been
approached by a young native lad, who asked him,
   'You shooting?'
   'Yes. Filming, yes.'
   'You from Granada.'
   'TV, yes. Yes I am. How did you know?'

'You know Tim.'
'Well, yes, I do. Yes.'
'You see him?'
'When I get back to Simla, yes. Why?'
'When you see him, you give him this, please.'

Nick had been entrusted a small roll of silk. He layed it on the bed, and gently unrolled it.

It was, to my disbelief and joy, a painting of an elephant, for Tom, and it had been painted and given to Nick by none other than Dinesh Sharma.

from *India Brittanica* by Geoffrey Moorhouse (1983)

When I reached India at last I was, like everyone else going there for the first time, intoxicated by the strangeness of this new experience. And yet, in the midst of its strangeness, and its towering scale of people and events, there was a haunting familiarity awaiting an Englishman there. Every visit I subsequently made to India was to confirm what I had only conjectured before I first went there; that the history of the British in India is something more than an account of conquest and submission, of rebellion and imperial retreat. It is also the story of a complicated love-hate relationship that no other two peoples so vastly different in origins and cultures, have ever known. Indians must speak for themselves about the relationship today. But they should know their country haunts the British still as nowhere else ever did, as no other place in the future possibly can.

Acknowledgements

These poems have been reprinted by kind permission of the following:

'Raj' by John Cotton, from *Kilroy Was Here*, published by Chatto & Windus; 'Routine' by Keki Daruwalla; 'To my Daughter Rookzain', 'Love among the Pines', and 'The Mistress' by Keki Daruwalla, published by Oxford University Press in New Delhi; 'Consummation' by Nissim Ezekiel; 'Night of the Scorpion', 'Marriage', 'The Patriot' and 'Poverty Poem' by Nissim Ezekiel, published by Oxford University Press in New Delhi; 'Indian Women' by Shiv Kumar; 'Mahabilipuram' by Louis MacNeice, reprinted by kind permission of Faber & Faber Ltd from *Collected Poems of Louis MacNeice*; 'Continuities' and 'A Letter to a Friend' by Arvind Krishna Mehrotra, from *Middle Earth*, published by Oxford University Press in New Delhi; 'The City Reels under the Heavy Load' by R. Parthasarathy, published by Oxford University Press in New Delhi; 'The Grove of the Perfect Being', 'Bengal', 'The Taj Express', '7/1 Burdwan Road, Calcutta' and 'The Gateway of India' by Alan Ross; and, through the office of Bonnie R. Crown, International Literature and Arts Program, permission has been arranged for the use of 'A Village Girl' by Mohan Singh.

These extracts have been reprinted by kind permission of the following:

Hindu Holiday by J. R. Ackerley (Arnold-Heinemann); *The Siege of Krishnaipur* by J. G. Farrell (Weidenfeld & Nicolson Ltd); *Freedom at Midnight* by Dominique Lapierre and Larry Collins (Grafton Books – a division of the Collins Publishing Group); 'The Mahratta Ghats', taken from *Ha! Ha! among the Trumpets* by Alun Lewis (Allen & Unwin Ltd); *The Lord of the Dance* by Robin Lloyd-Jones (Victor Gollancz Ltd); *India Britannica* by Geoffrey Moorhouse (Collins Publishers); and *The Raj Quartet* by Paul Scott (Heinemann Ltd).

All definitions in this anthology are based on those in *Harper's Dictionary of Hinduism*.

Index